Prevention of Dementia

A book based on Ayurveda, Yoga and other
preventive methods

Dr. Vinod Verma

Prevention of Dementia

A book based on Ayurveda, Yoga and other preventive methods

Gayatri Books International

Disclaimer

This book is written for healthy people for adopting a way of life that coordinates with the natural cosmic order so that they can prevent a deadly disorder like Dementia. Material provided in this book is not to replace the services of a physician or to provide healing when the disease is already there. The purpose of this book is to provide knowledge about dementia and healthy ways of living for its prevention. No medical claims by the author or the publisher will be accepted in this direction.

To use the remedies provided in this book for commercial purpose, written permission and agreement from the author are required. For more information, write to the author directly at ayurvedavv@yahoo.com or ayurvedavv@gmail.com

Visit Dr. Vinod Verma at www.ayurvedavv.com and www.books.drvinodverma.com to find out about her other publications and activities like seminars, lectures, consultations, etc. Look for more information on the last pages of the book.

Cover design and photographs by: Mohit Joshi and the author
Edited by Dr. Aruna Sattanathan Pillai

ISBN: 978-81-89514-15-0

Contents

This book is dedicated to my Ayurveda Guru

Late Acharya Priya Vrat Sharma

Who devoted his life for spreading Ayurvedic wisdom.

His numerous works are the continuous source of guidance for

me and millions of others.

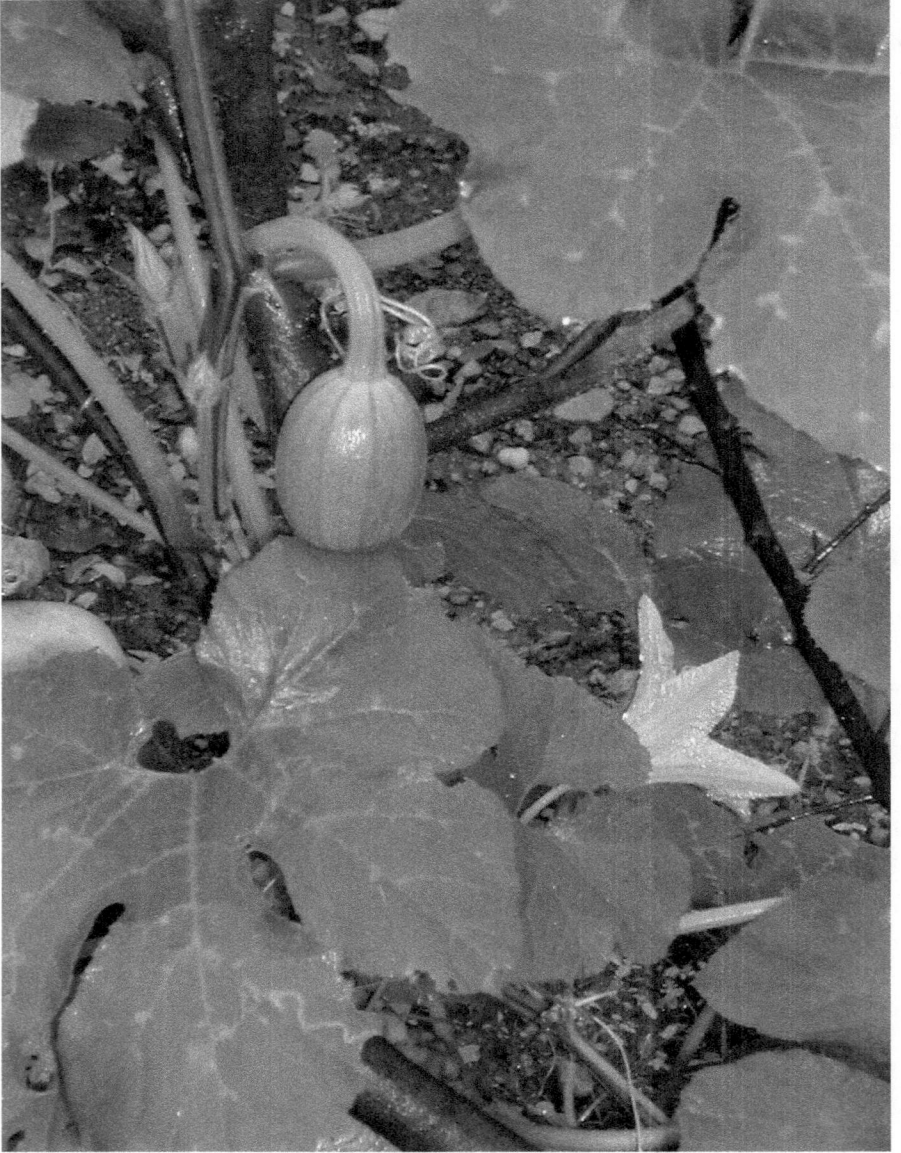

Foreword

It is a basic fact that Dementia is spreading like wild fire all over the world. At the moment, the higher percentage of dementia patients are found in the economically affluent societies of the world (see map in Wikipedia). However, in the developing countries, its spread is directly proportionate to affluence and adopting a mindset based on the mind-dominating philosophy. In brief, it is the lifestyle and the attitude, which is associated with the industrialisation and the Western philosophy of a mind's domination over body. Descartes' philosophy of attributing all the powers of a being to the mind and considering it as 'self' has done tremendous harm. That has lead to the misuse of mind and thus deformation of its capabilities.

For preventing the horrors of dementia in future, along with the lifestyle, we need to change our attitude and learn to coordinate our mind with the five senses and the physiological body. We should stop being only a 'mind individual' but a whole being whose real self is not mind but an energy that puts life into a body of which mind is only a part.

Dr. Verma has very logically explained the reasons of the rapid spread of dementia in our times and has provided a list of twelve major risk factors leading to dementia. They are both at physical and mental level. Avoidance of these risk factors can save humanity from the gradual destruction of the human mind. Considering that dementia occurs due to various mental disorders and loss of memory is an irreversible change, prevention seems to be the best solution. It is our dharma, as human beings to safeguard our body and mind. Thus, the dimension of prevention Dr. Verma is taking is based on individual effort. This work will be beneficial for humanity at large.

Prof. Dharmanand Sharma
Department of Philosophy
Panjab University, Chandigarh, India

Preface

Diseases like cardiac ailments, hypertension, backaches, mental disorders, diabetes, brain haemorrhages are increasing at an alarming rate in the modern world. The most prominent and uncontrollably spreading mental disorder throughout the world is dementia. Dementia is indicated by gradual loss of memory along with the cognitive, functional and emotional problems. It is the result of diverse disorders in the brain. In advanced stages of the disease, the patient is handicapped and needs emotional and physical care.

Landmark data from the World Health Organization (WHO) reveals that around the world a new case of dementia occurs every four seconds. That is the equivalent of 7.7 million new cases each year. In the words of global health expert Dr. Peter Piot, dementia is a 'ticking time bomb.' The number of people living with dementia worldwide is currently estimated at 35.6 million. This number will double by 2030 and more than triple by 2050.

If there will be so many patients suffering from this disorder in less then 20 years, who will take care of whom? It is time that we begin to work on the prevention of this deadly ailment in a rigorous manner, especially when there is practically no treatment available. At the moment most of the efforts and finances in research are concentrated on treatment. This book is written with the purpose of preventing dementia with personal efforts and diverse measures taken at individual level to avoid the 'trouble not yet come'. Since this is an age related disorder in most cases, we should work on its prevention from younger years.

The ancient Indian medical wisdom from the Vedas places a great emphasis on prevention of ailments and more than 85 percent of Ayurveda is on

11

healthy living, preventing ailments and rejuvenating the body to work against ageing. Living with time and space and leading a life with inner peace and stillness is emphasized. Intake of several rejuvenating products and various other activities to strengthen each and every part of the body are described to prevent the ailments, which are associated with wear and tear of aging and/or are caused by our misdeeds. We commit these mistakes due to lack of fundamental and holistic knowledge about our body and its relationship to the cosmos.

The book describes specific features leading to dementia and ways to avoid these in order to prevent this dreadful disorder. The figures stated above about the increase of this disorder are often discussed in the media and instigate a great fear in the public. However, there are no guidelines issued to teach people about its prevention and there are no clear views on this subject in the public health departments. Scientists are busy doing research to find a cure for this ailment but not much attention is paid to its prevention. The existing preventive methods offered by modern scientific research are non-holistic, depend on very small sample size and are simplistic. Most of them are arbitrary and vague. For example— eat a healthy diet or drink moderate quantity of alcohol everyday. Another study suggests eating walnuts regularly for preventing dementia and yet another recommends laughing yoga. It is also recommended to use your brain more for prevention of dementia. This sounds particularly ironical, as it is observed that even high level intellectuals are known to get this disorder.

All of us need to question ourselves as to what is leading us to senility at a pandemic scale. Why did it not happen a few generations ago? Where have we erred? Can we stop this up coming disaster? This book is meant to make you aware of various risk factors leading to this deadly disorder and ways to prevent the senility related to aging. The more risk factors you have, more the chances of your getting dementia. Each risk factor is explained, as also the ways to eliminate it. The process of learning the right way to live involves learning wisdom about life. Taking preventive measures for dementia suggested in this book will also improve your quality of life and will enhance your energy level as well.

Vinod Verma   October 2011
www.ayurvedavv.com
www.books.drvinodverma.com
ayurvedavv@yahoo.com

Acknowledgements

I express my profound gratitude to Professor Dharmanand Sharma for inspiring discussions from philosophical point of view on the theme of dementia. I am also grateful to him for writing the foreword for this book. This theme particularly is moving for both of us, as we have a professor colleague and friend who is suffering from this ailment.

I am highly appreciative of Dr. Aruna Sattanathan Pillai for her painstaking effort to edit this book. Aruna is a very talented editor and has edited this book with great involvement and love.

The idea to write this book was born in Germany during a lecture in October 2011 in Munich where my worthy German editor-in-Chief Sabine Jaenicke was present. The lecture was on *The Lifestyle disorders and their Prevention with Ayurveda.* Someone in the audience asked me a question specifically on the prevention of Dementia, which I replied by telling about the risk factors that lead to dementia and how one can take care to prevent these factors. As soon as the lecture finished, Sabine asked me to write this book immediately. Strangely, few weeks before that, Brigitte Keil in Dresden from the Chamber of Pharmacist in Saxony had asked me to speak on prevention of Dementia in a seminar in May 2012 for their organisation. This much needed book took its form with these events and I am grateful to all these three ladies who lead me to treat this topic immediately, which is indispensible for public awareness and public health.

I am also grateful to Eckhard and Andie Biermann in Freiburg for providing me a home in Germany and supporting my research.

1

Dementia and its Causes: A view of Modern Science and Medicine

Dementia is a Latin word which means madness or mindlessness. *De* means without and *ment* means mind. In the present medical context, dementia is the loss of mind's cognitive ability. The symptoms are a gradual loss of memory and ability to coordinate thoughts and actions.

Dementia is not a name for a particular disease but it is the result of diverse ailments that affect the functions of the mind and result in loss of memory and cognition. Dementia is also termed in common language as senility which occurs through ageing.

Following are the four principal disorders that lead to dementia.

- **Dementia due to Alzheimer's disease:** Small clumps of protein begin to develop around brain cells and disrupt the normal working of the brain leading to dementia. This disease is the major cause of dementia in the world.
- **Vascular dementia:** This is caused due to the problems in blood circulation. Parts of the brain do not receive enough blood and oxygen, thereby causing disruption in normal functions of the brain.
- **Dementia with Lewy bodies**: This is caused due to some abnormal protein structures, known as Lewy bodies, which develop inside the brain.

- **Fronto-temporal dementia**: This is caused due to the shrinkage in the frontal and temporal lobes of the brain.

Besides these four major causes of dementia, any other ailment that leads to damaging of the brain cells in one way or the other will lead to dementia. It may be due to a disease like AIDS, some obstruction in blood circulation (arteriosclerosis) and high blood pressure (hypertension), some brain infections like virus or parasite, constant mental tension and pressure, etc.

In other words, we can say that dementia results from deformation, damage or death of the nerve cells in the brain due to diverse reasons.

Symptoms of Dementia

Dementia is a syndrome (a group of related symptoms) that is associated with an ongoing decline of the brain and its abilities. These include:

- Lack of coherent thinking
- Gradual loss of memory
- Confusion in speech and language
- Decrease in understanding of simple things
- Inaccuracy in coordination and judgment

People with dementia may have problems controlling their emotions and therefore they behave inappropriately in social situations. Others perceive changes in various aspects of their personality due to the above causes or they may see or hear things that other people do not, or have false beliefs.

Most cases of dementia are caused by damage to the structure of the brain. People with dementia usually need help from friends or relatives, including help in making decisions. The conditions usually develop slowly. Three main types of symptoms can appear:

- Cognitive problems – it gets harder to understand, remember, think, do sums, learn new things, talk or make judgements
- Functional problems – it gets hard to do complicated tasks. As time goes on, it gets harder to do the basic task of looking after oneself, like washing and dressing.
- Emotional problems– the mood can change, the patient may lose emotional control, stop doing things that she or he enjoyed and stop seeing people.

With aging, these symptoms enhance to such an extent that the patients may forget their own identity, forget to cater to their natural urges like hunger, thirst, excretion, etc. The patient may not remember whether he or she has already taken food and may begin to eat again. During the last stages of this ailment, the patient is handicapped and needs 24 hours attendance and care.

Mental and behavioural disorders represent four of the ten leading causes of disability worldwide, and they are estimated to account for 12% of the global burden of disease (WHO, 2001). European and North American studies show that about one-fourth of the population above age 65 suffers from mental health problems. About 6 to 10 percent have severe dementia and severe functional losses.

The number of people suffering from dementia worldwide is currently estimated to be 35.6 million. This number will double by 2030 and more than triple by 2050. According to some other estimate from Kings College London, 115 million people will suffer from dementia across the globe by 2050.

Treatment

There are no cures, as yet for dementia or in other words to treat the principal ailments that lead to dementia. However, some drugs are known to arrest the course of degeneration. Acetyl cholinesterase inhibitors may slow the progression of Alzheimer's dementia and Lewy Body dementia. Another drug called memantine, a glutamate blocker, may protect brain cells against damage. In Vascular dementia and possibly Alzheimer's, other drugs that enhance blood circulation may be used to slow down the damage to brain cells.

2

Dementia: A Holistic View

Let us try to first understand the major causes of dementia according to the ancient Indian medical system from the Vedas. The written Vedic medical tradition began from the last or fourth Veda called the *Atharva* Veda, estimated to be about 6000 years old. Later around 1000 B.C. the medical wisdom was more refined and compiled in the form of a fifth Veda— the Ayurveda. Ayurveda is in fact the most ancient medical system of the world and is the mother medical system of all the existing systems. According to this ancient holistic science of life, the entire universe works on the same fundamental principles. All living (*chetan*) and non-living (*jadda*) things are made of five fundamental elements. *Chetan* differs from *jadda* for having an independent system (smaller system within the bigger cosmic system) whereas the *jadda* is a part of the bigger cosmic system. The equilibrium of the five elements in the cosmos speaks for harmony and their imbalance leads to catastrophes. *Chetan* have independent micro-cosmos where the five elements form the three principal energies for performing the functions of this system. In human beings, all the functions of the body and the mind are performed by these three principal energies (dosha) and they should be kept in balance with conscious effort by taking right nutrition, living according to space and time, proper breathing, sufficient body movements and living with the rhythm of nature. The imbalance is generally due to anti-natural lifestyle that leads to ill health and suffering.

The body, mind and senses

Since in the present context, we are dealing with a mental ailment, let me explain how the body mind and self are viewed in this holistic tradition. The physical body comprises of five senses and the mind. Mind is considered as the coordinator of the senses. In fact, it is considered as the sixth and the most superior of all the senses. Without mind, its coordinating ability and its sense of discretion (the buddhi), senses are rendered ineffectual and inadequate. But above the senses and the mind is that invisible energy (soul), which is the cause of being and is the real self of an individual. This philosophy of existence is different from the Western view from seventeenth century onwards, where mind is generally considered as the 'self' of an individual and is supreme.

To put these concepts in simple words, in the Vedic tradition, the soul is the continuity of a human being, as it is not destroyed by death. It is mere energy, which is not material or sensual. That means it cannot be touched, seen or felt. However this energy is the living element of the mind and the senses that constitute the physical being of an individual and it expresses itself through the physical being.

Some of you may not be familiar with the Ayurvedic principles and therefore, for a better understanding, I give below in the box some essential features of three energies of the body.

The Dynamics of the Body

There is a principle of uniformity in nature. Everything that exists is constituted of five elements. Five elements in the cosmos are dynamic and well coordinated and form a perfect system. The sun brings us warmth and light each day and the darkness of the night is beautified with stars and changing phases of the moon. There are clouds, rains, snow and the rivers are gushing towards their destination. With the dynamism of the five elements, seeds become sprouts; trees lose their leaves and get new ones. The living being from both plant and animal world die and new life comes to being. There is no still moment in this dynamic cosmos and change is another name for time. Nothing is lost and there is constant transformation.

Like the cosmos, an individual living system is also perfect and dynamic. It is a part of the cosmos and likewise it is constituted of the five fundamental elements. But the elements in a living system are present in the form of three energies or dosha in order to perform all the functions of this particular system. To perform all the mental and physical functions of the body, the three energies coordinate with each other and make a perfect system. The body has further smaller systems or organisms, which perform their individual functions, and the three energies also coordinate these functions. These energies are called vata, pitta and kapha in the technical language of Ayurveda and each has specific functions with the characteristics of the elements they are derived from.

Dynamics of three energies or dosha: vata, pitta and kapha

Vata is constituted from elements ether and air and its functions are related to these two elements. Ether or space is omnipresent and air is mobile. The functions related to movements as well as to space are performed by vata.

Vata is responsible for entire body movements, blood circulation, respiration, excretion, functions related to nerves and brain, speech, sensations, touch, hearing, feelings like fear, anxiety, grief, enthusiasm etc., natural urges, formation of foetus, sexual act and retention.

21

Fire constitutes pitta energy of the body and thus pitta is body's fire or *agni*. When we use the word *agni* in Ayurveda, it pertains to everything related to digestion and assimilation. *Agni* in Ayurvedic terminology is a part of pitta but as you see pitta has also some other functions.

Pitta is responsible for vision, hunger, thirst, heat regulation, softness, lustre, cheerfulness, intellect, mental lucidity and sexual vigour.

Kapha forms the solid part of the body and is responsible for the formation of new cells. Also when we are adult, our body constantly needs new cells. We need various secretions in the body. The inner lining of the digestive system and uterus are constantly renewed.

Kapha constitutes all the solid structure of the body and is responsible for binding different body organs together. It gives rise to firmness and heaviness to the body and is responsible for sexual potency, strength, forbearance and restraint.

Due to external influences like cosmic changes, diverse life situations, geographical conditions, time (in terms of time of the day, time of the year and one's age), the balance of these energies keeps changing but it reverts back to normal by natural means. If human beings do anti-natural acts, make perverted or negative use of their senses, eat antagonistic foods and not follow the rhythm of nature, they fall prey to imbalance of the fundamental energies. Imbalance of one or more energies disturbs the functional system of the body and if left unattended, it becomes chronic and gives rise to numerous disorders related to the imbalance of that particular energy. The first duty of human beings (*svadharma*) is to live in tune with nature, according to space and time and do everything to maintain the fundamental balance of the body to prevent ailments. They should strengthen the body by taking rejuvenating products (rasayana) and to live with an optimum level of energy until old age. Equally important is to maintain mental balance, live with a sense of contentment (*santosha*) and use yogic means to obtain stillness of mind (sattva).

Prevention and treatment of mental disorders in Ayurveda

For a better understanding of the prevention of dementia and the methods given in this book, I would like to provide you some fundamental features of therapy used in Ayurveda for treating the ailments of the head region (mental and brain disorders, sinusitis, weakness or ailments of senses, falling and greying of hair, etc.).

1. Treatment is given with brain and nerve strengthening medications, like brahmi, aindri, jyotishmati, long pepper, and so on. Various rasayanas are prepared with these drugs and are given orally. Medicated oils are also prepared from these drugs for external applications like massage, *shirobasti* or *shirodhara*.

2. Nasya treatment, which is a part of panchakarma or the five purification practices, is given with special medicated oils or herbal powders through nasal passage. Nose is considered the gateway of the head and the medications induced through nasal passage open the channels in the head, improve the oxygenation and hence the functioning of the brain. Similarly, various odours have an important role in therapy. The popular aromatherapy of modern times is developed from Ayurvedic wisdom. To treat mental

ailments in Ayurveda, various kinds of herbs are burnt and their smoke (*dhooni*) is inhaled.

3. The third principal therapy is the hyper hydration of the head region with medicated oils which contain brain rejuvenating herbs. There are several ways to do it. Special head massage with oil is called *champi* (the word shampoo originates from it). There is a technique of holding plenty of oil in the centre of the scalp and it is called *shirobasti*. Another technique which was developed in Kerala is called *Shirodhara* that involves pouring medicated oil on the forehead and letting it flow backwards on the whole scalp. This is a very popular technique amongst westerners, as today's stressed people get great relief with it.

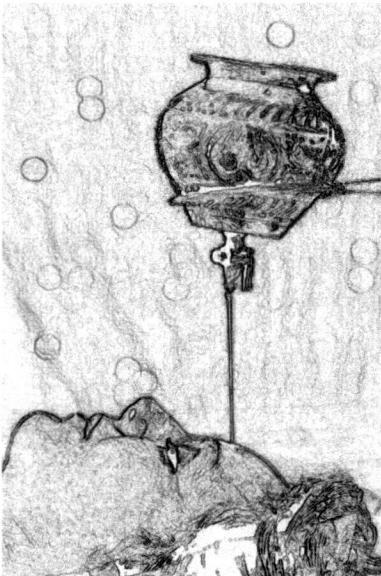 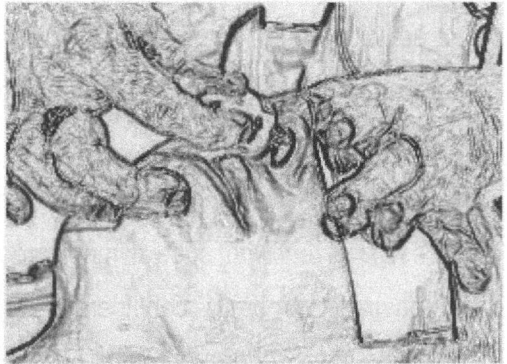

Shirodhara   Nasya

The five cleansing practices of Ayurveda along with fat therapy and massage invigorate the body and save us from ailments and disorders. They are recommended twice a year during the change of major seasons (October and March on the Northern Hemisphere). I have provided simple methods to do these on your own at home in my book— *Programming Your Life with Ayurveda.*

Brain, nerves and mind

Five elements constituting the body make three principal energies for performing all the physical and mental functions. Let us see which energy performs the functions of the brain like perception, cognition, thought process and memory.

- Ether and air are the first two elements which form vata energy that perform all the functions which are agile and involve movement. The brain and nerve functions and cognition are the functions performed by Vata energy.

- The third element is fire that forms pitta energy and performs the functions of metabolism, vision, clarity of thought and creativity.

- The last two elements are water and earth and they form kapha energy, which is like the building material of the body. Growth, formation of new cells, glandular secretions are some of the principal functions of this energy.

In normal living conditions, mind is constantly processing the knowledge obtained from five senses and is always active. During sleep, the five senses are partially closed and the mind is closed to new knowledge. Nevertheless, the mind is processing old knowledge, which is stored in the form of memory.

Mind is constantly undergoing modification, as its thinking process has a ceaseless chain of thoughts, called *chitta* in Sanskrit. We go back to the Yoga Guru Patanjali to understand a little more about the functioning of the mind. He analysed the mind's modification into five categories: evidence, misconception, fancy, sleep and memory. These five types of modifications can be either afflictive or non-afflictive. I cite below some details about the modifications of mind from my book *Patanjali and Ayurvedic Yoga.*

1. **Evidence:** We perceive something through our senses. The object perceived is imprinted on our mind with its form, colour, smell etc. The second step is that the mind cognises that image of the object and infers its identity (whether it is a river, a mountain, a cow, a tree or a table, and so on). The inference depends upon testimony. I call a stone a stone or a tree a tree because others before me have done it. It is important to understand that these three steps of modification of the mind are distinct from each other. I perceive a table and infer it according to the previous knowledge that it is a table. My perception is different from the reality of the table. They are two distinct things. I call this thing with four legs and a flat top a table because others before me have decided to do so. I distinguish a table from a bed although they are similar in their fundamental form but different in shape and size. That means that I have certain beliefs as what a table should be and what a bed should be. All this may sound like an unnecessary discussion to some of you, but it is important to comprehend these differences in order to achieve the stillness of the mind. When these three stages of evidence become one for a person, the mind attains stillness. For example, if I fix my mind on the reality of the table, that is, the mass, shape and form of the table, forgetting about its name and image in my mind, the first step is achieved by hindering the modifications of the mind. Try this exercise with different objects around you and you will have this experience. For example, go to a quiet garden, stay at a fair distance from a tree and just concentrate on the form of the tree forgetting all about its name and other knowledge about it. That means, you are only visually absorbing the form of the tree and are not letting your mind wander about inferring and

---

* *Patanjali and Ayurvedic Yoga*, Gayatri Books International. Latest edition is available at www.amazon.com

testifying this sensuous experience of visualising a tree. This is a very simple method to attain a thought-free mind at least for a short interval.

2. **Misconception:** It is an incorrect notion that does not reveal the real nature of the object concerned. This modification of the mind may occur at various levels. One may mistake a night-light for moon, plastic plants for the real ones, mirage of the desert for water, and so on. At another level, one may interpret the noise of leaves for a tiger while walking in the forest. Some fainted person may be mistaken for dead and an already dead person may be considered as still alive. To believe the false as truth and what is real and true, as false is another example of mistaken notion or misconception.

3. **Fancy:** This is the knowledge conveyed by words and is devoid of an object. Thoughts like imagination about the future, heaven, hell, projecting oneself to be rich, fearing oneself to be poor, and so on are in this category. The abstract concepts like '*Purusha* and *Prakriti* together are the cause of phenomenal world', 'our future is decided from our past and present *karma*', 'the universe is an ever-changing and dynamic whole', and so on, are the modifications of the mind which come in the category of fancy.

4. **Sleep:** It is that modification, which occurs in the absence of new knowledge, as the senses are temporarily closed to the external world during sleep. All the sense organs and organs of action are in an inert stage during sleep. However, the modifications of the mind go on during sleep. There are dreams during sleep, which can be recalled after waking up. Even if one may think that the sleep was without dreams, one is still aware of the kind of sleep one had– like sound sleep, restless sleep etc. The mental processes do not stop during sleep despite the fact that the sensory perception is considerably reduced. I have used the word 'reduced', as it is not totally closed because during sleep, if there is a loud noise or a strong smell or too much light or someone touches us, we wake up.

5. **Memory:** It is the retention of notion we have already had. Due to memory, our thought process is constantly occupied. It is my theory that we never forget anything. Everything is stored in our minds but certain memories are suppressed or stacked in the profounder layers. For example, when we see a person, who was with us in the kindergarten or primary school thirty years ago, our mind starts to search and tries to place that known face. We generally end up recognising and remembering the person concerned. Besides this kind of dormant memory, we have active thoughts from the recent past. Thus, our mind is often occupied with events, which are based on memory and this modification of mind along with the present perception makes the regular chain of thoughts in the mind.

Pain and pleasure from the five modifications

The five kinds of modifications of the mind are either afflictive or non-afflictive. They may bring us pain or may not bring us pain. In fact, whether they bring us pain or pleasure in the normal sense of the world, they will come under the category of afflictive. The material and sensuous pleasures do not remain constant in this ever-changing dynamic world. The departure of pleasure is also pain. In the present context, non-afflictive will be those modifications of the mind, which lead one to wisdom of recognising one's real self, soul as distinct from the destructible and perishable physical self.

For strengthening the mind by giving it rest, we need to make an effort to stop the modifications from time to time. The thought process of the mind is called *chitta* in Sanskrit. *Chitta* has a compulsive nature (*vriti*) to have a constant chain of thoughts. However, we human being have a capability of stopping these chain of thoughts and are able to concentrate on a single point. Mind controls mind and by doing that we open the higher faculties and capabilities of our mind. The whole scenario of human existence is described very beautifully in *Katha* Upanisha.

The body is like a chariot

of which soul is the owner

the intellect is its driver

the mind plays the part of reins,

as for the horses, those are the senses,

the world is their arena.

It is the intellect (the driver) which should lead the horses (senses) by using the reins (the mind), along with its owner, the soul to the destination.

In the Vedic tradition, the fundamentals of human existence are quite the opposite to those of Descartes and the other thinkers of that time. 'I am (due to the presence of my soul in my body), therefore I can think' is totally opposite to 'I think, therefore I am'.

In our times, there is over use of senses, exhaustion of mind and exploitation of human capabilities due to commercialisation of everything. We misuse our mental faculties by enforcing the mind-based existence, which ignores the body on one hand and hinders the mental development on the other hand. An alarming rise in dementia shows that not only have we destroyed our environment and nature, we have also destroyed the human mind.

In the world of hyper-activities, the body is ignored and its primary balance is disturbed. The natural urges like hunger, excretion and sleep are disturbed. From physical to mental level, there is chaos. The mental faculties can take this turmoil only to a certain extent and ultimately they give up and withdraw. This is what is dementia.

The thinking process of the mind has three characteristic qualities (guna): quality related to activities (rajas), quality that hinders action (tamas) and quality of peace and stillness (sattva). The activities of the mind like planning, organising, etc. are the rajas qualities. Senses and mind are active and are in coordination with each other. When these faculties are fatigued, the senses and mind reach the state of tamas or inaction. Tamas includes those thoughts which hinder our inner development. These are rivalry, jealousy, anger, hatred, distress, discontentment, grumbling, etc. These are popularly called negative thoughts.

Sattva is the state of stillness and peace. It is a state when modifications of the mind or the chain of thoughts are slowed down and quietened. A state of concentration on a single object or a sound or beholding the beauty of nature or devotion to God or gods, or realisation one's real self as soul help quieten the mind and bring a sattva state. Worldly activities generally comprise of rajas and tamas and sattva is the balancing factor for these. Lack of sattva or the inner peace and stillness leads to disorders, as it affects both body and mind.

Body, mind and mental disorders

Earlier it has been said that the body is constituted of five fundamental elements and that they form three principal energies to perform all the physical and mental functions of the body and mind. The brain and nerve functions, blood circulation, the functions related to movements are performed by vata energy formed from ether and air. A chronic imbalance of this energy leads to many ailments related to the functions of this energy. Out of the numerous disorders of chronic vata imbalance or *vikriti*, Charaka has described eighty prominent ones in *Sutrasthana*. There are some disorders amongst them, which are related to brain and nerves and thus are the precursors of a bigger disorder like shrinkage of temporal lobes, Alzheimer or other related disorders leading to dementia. These vata disorders are:

 a) Frequent pain in the temporal regions and other parts of the body
 b) frequent delirium (*atipralap* in Sanskrit which means often indulging in incoherent and nonsensical talk)
 c) instability of mind (*anavasthitchita*)

There are other symptoms during excessive vata imbalance like *chittabhrama* (delusion), *gyanbhranti* (misconception), *chaitnyanasha* (destruction at the level of awareness and consciousness).

From the above description, it is clear that the root cause of ailments leading to dementia has precursors in chronic vata imbalance: However, the reader should be aware that, there are numerous disorders due to chronic vata imbalance and which disorder one gets depends upon different factors like the life history of a person, fundamental constitution, geographical location, lifestyle and food habits. Various aches and pains (headaches, knee, back and shoulder are the most common these days), arthritis, hypertension, various disorders related to circulatory system, several ailments of the heart, stiffness of body, ears or eyes, loss of hearing, nervousness and delirium are some of the major disorders caused due to chronic vata. In the context of dementia, I can state that the key factors lie in vata imbalance and the theme of prevention of dementia is based upon the fundamental mind-body balance. It is also important for the reader to know that imbalance any one of the energies, if left unattended for a long time, ultimately causes the imbalance of all the energies. The three energies work in tandem. More of this is described in the eighth chapter.

Delirium is considered differently in the modern science and medicine. It is treated as an independent disorder and not as a precursor of ailments leading to dementia. Given below are the definition and symptoms of delirium described in ADAM Medical Encyclopaedia. I have highlighted those symptoms, which, in my opinion are directly related to dementia, and are the pre-symptoms of this disorder.

"Delirium is most often caused by physical or mental illness and is usually temporary and reversible. Many disorders cause delirium, including conditions that deprive the brain of oxygen or other substances.

Symptoms

- Changes in feeling (sensation) and perception
- **Changes in level of consciousness or awareness**
- Changes in movement (for example, may be slow moving or hyperactive)
- Changes in sleep patterns, drowsiness
- **Confusion (disorientation) about time or place**
- **Decrease in short-term memory and recall**
  - Unable to remember events since delirium began (anterograde amnesia)
  - Unable to remember events before delirium (retrograde amnesia)
- **Disrupted or wandering attention**
  - Inability to think or behave with purpose
  - **Problems concentrating**
- **Disorganized thinking**
  - **Speech that doesn't make sense (incoherent)**
  - Inability to stop speech patterns or behaviours".

Existing Western medical literature further emphasizes that delirium is not a disease but a syndrome. It is very frequent in hospitalized patients. "Delirium is probably the single most common acute disorder affecting adults in general hospitals. It affects 10-20% of all hospitalized adults, and 30-40% of elderly hospitalized patients and up to 80% of ICU patients."*

From our traditional Ayurvedic wisdom, the experts state that most allopathic medications lead to extreme vata imbalance. In Ayurveda, to treat delirium or to treat the side-effects of allopathic medications, we treat vata by giving

---

* Ely EW, Shintani A, Truman B, et al. (2004). *JAMA* **291** (14): 1753–62.. doi:10.1001/jama.291.14.1753. PMID 15082703.

32

oil massages, heat application, unctuous nutrition and some other simple self-help products. Unctuous food in Ayurveda means the food prepared with an appropriate quantity of oil or ghee or butter. Unctuous measures means application of oils on the body with massage or intake of ghee or some other prescribed fat orally to soften the internal organs. Besides that, we detoxify the body with various herbal combinations and purification practices called *panchkarma*.

In the late eighties, in my first book on Ayurveda, while describing vata and its imbalance, I had said that the modern way of living is vata oriented. There is too much action, movement, thinking, organisation and above all food with long shelf life, grown with artificial fertilizers and sprayed with pesticides. There is competition, jealousy and greed to own more and more. The body and mind are not given real rest and even holidays or leisure time is overloaded with hectic routines. There is a lack of what brings peace to mind and body— *santosha* or the sense of contentment. In fact, Charaka has gone so far to say that *asantosha* or the sense of being dissatisfied is the root cause of most ailments. All this leads to vata imbalance, which becomes chronic and intense over a period of time leading first to fatigue and exhaustion and ultimately delirium and mental instability. However, until this stage, the process is reversible with appropriate treatment, rest and a change in lifestyle and thinking (*achara-vyavhar*).

Chronic vata imbalance ⟹ Delirium and Instability of mind
When left unattended ⟹ Disorders leading to dementia

For preventing dementia, we have to make an effort to eradicate the precursors of this disorder. The principal factors are chronic vata imbalance and disequilibrium in mental qualities due to lack of sattva or inner stillness and harmony. The details of these will be explained in later chapters of the book.

3

Principal risk factors leading to Dementia

No ailment or disorder appears suddenly in the body. It is caused gradually due to diverse physical and mental imbalances built over a number of years. The three fundamental energies of the body are responsible for physical and mental functions. It is our duty (*svadharma*) to maintain the balance of these three energies, as well as of the three characteristic qualities of the mind to maintain good health.

The three states of mind and the three energies of the body mutually influence each other. An imbalance of vata gives a hectic and nervous state of mind causing rajas imbalance. The imbalanced rajas further disturbs vata. Similarly, an imbalance of kapha energy leads to inertia and thus gives rise to too much tamas. Too much tamasic action like excessive sleep, inertia, feeling of heaviness, inaction, passive lifestyle, etc., lead to imbalance of kapha. Sattva is the inner light of an individual and pitta is the warmth and energy of the body. It is related to intellect and clarity. Sattva is the spiritual lucidity.

For preventing dementia, a horrific ailment, which is attacking us on a pandemic scale, we will have to systematically understand the multidimensional factors that put us at risk. The key features are to bring about equilibrium in the way of living, maintaining balance in the six dimensions of our being and strengthening the mind with sattva (see chapter 7 for more details).

Given below are the twelve major risk factors. The remedial methods are described in the next chapter. The more risk factors you have, the more the chances of your getting dementia. The longer you have lived with these risk factors, the more hard you will have to work to eradicate them.

Risk factors for dementia

Risk Factor 1

Excessive and negative use of senses

> **Perverted, negative and excessive use of sense objects, time and intellect (buddhi) is the three-fold cause of both mental and physical disorders. Both body and mind are the location of disorders, as well as of pleasure. Their balanced use is the cause of pleasure**[*]

The above citation from Charaka clearly states that the five senses, mind, and the capacity to discriminate and decide (buddhi) should be used appropriately to avoid mental and physical disorders. In the present context of dementia, the principal concern is with the sense of hearing and its object sound. This sense is related to air and space elements. Speaking loudly or too much or hearing people or sounds which are loud, unnecessary or unwanted affect your nerves and exhaust them. If it is your routine to be a part of this exhausting and noisy atmosphere, they will have an ill effect on you in the long run. The principle of life is that exhaustion (excessive rajas) leads to withdrawal, inertia (tamas) and suspended action of that particular organ. Ultimately, the organ develops a sub-system which is not in rhythm with the rest of the system and that is what is a major disorder.[**]

---

[*] *Charka Samhita, Sutrasthana*, 1, 54-55

Imagine a mother of two children who works as a secretary or as a manager where she has to deal with many phone calls and many visitors. Besides that, she has to organise the house and spend the evenings with her little children catering to their needs and demands. If she has a husband who is unable to share the load at home, it is too much for her. She is over-using her senses and has no real rest. Such are the vulnerable cases.

There are people who speak needlessly loudly, even on the phone. There are others for whom the raised volume is symbolic of their higher status. With mobile phones where the sound is amplified several times, loud speaking is unnecessarily stressful for ears and nerves and fatigues the mind. Similarly, listening to loud music or always having radio, television or other devices on for music or sound fatigues the sense of hearing, and ultimately has ill effects on body and mind.

Risk Factor 2

Incorrect shoulder and neck posture

Incorrect posture with forward bent shoulders and curved cervical vertebrae hinder the blood flow to the brain and thus over a long period of time lead to disorders. A curve in the seven cervical vertebrae (neck vertebrae) hinders the passage of arteries, veins, lymphs and nerves and cause hindrance in free flow of energy, primarily diminishing the blood supply to the brain. The brain has high metabolism and high requirements of blood. It is estimated that 15% of the cardiac output is used by the brain. I am not talking of ischemia or lack of blood flow, which causes cerebral cell death. I am talking

---

** For more details of system and subsystems, see the Appendix of my book *Ayurveda: A way of Life*. Latest edition is available at www.amazon.com.

of a situation where both the pressure and the quantity of blood supply are slightly affected and have a long-term effect on the brain.

Risk Factor 3

Incorrect Breathing

From Ayurvedic and yogic point of view, we not only breathe air (oxygen being an essential component of survival), but we take inside us the cosmic energy or prana with each breath. Breathing provides us the living element of the cosmos and keeps the connection between body and soul. As soon as the intake of air or prana or the cosmic living element stops, the soul (the cause of being) departs from the body and the life of an individual ends.

The prana energy or the air we breathe all our life, in fact provides us all the five elements of which the universe is constituted. It is like nourishment to the body and mind. When the breath is taken only halfway, we deprive ourselves of the cosmic energy and become prey to weakness and fatigue, as well as to mental and physical disorders. This gives a dull appearance, pale complexion and other signs of vata imbalance. If we get only half of our food requirements, we start to show signs of weakness and fatigue. Similarly, due to incorrect breathing (which is not deep and conscious), we get only half of our requirement of prana or the cosmic energy.

Risk Factor 4

Nasal Blockades

Constant phlegm in the nasal passages and a frequently blocked nose hinders the flow of air in the head region. If the flow is hindered, it affects the nerves and brain over a period of time, leading to sluggishness and dullness. It gives rise to lack of attention, diminished retention and memory.

Risk Factor 5

Chronic Cold, Excessive mucous in Head region and Sinusitis

Frequent attacks of cold and constant phlegm formation in your system that makes you blow your nose or spit it out are bad signs and indicate that the presence of phlegm makes blockades in your head region. The air-filled passages of the skull are called sinuses. In healthy conditions, they are able to drain out mucous. If the mucous accumulates in these cavities, bacteria and virus also develop there, giving rise to the pathological condition called sinusitis. This leads to symptoms like headache, fatigue, frequent cold and cough, fever, nasal congestion, etc. which spoils the inner climate of the upper region and badly affects the brain.

Risk Factor 6

A chronic imbalance of body's vital energies called vata

In the previous chapter, I have already stated that the three vital energies are responsible for performing all physical and mental functions of the body. The vata energy is responsible for brain and nerves. It is further stated that a chronic imbalance of vata gives rise to some ailments related to brain and nerves and amongst them the most prominent is delirium. In fact, vata imbalance is the biggest risk factor. Vata is formed from ether and air elements and all functions which are spread in space and involve movement are the functions of vata. Brain and nerve functions (central and peripheral nervous systems) are performed by vata energy. A chronic imbalance of this energy affects the functional capacity of the brain, thus, paving way for diverse disorders leading to dementia.

Risk factor 7

General body weakness, frequent bouts of fatigue and exhaustion

The general weakness in the body can be due to many reasons. It could be due to weak digestive fire (metabolism) and bad assimilation of food or bad food habits or too much physical labour, etc. Bouts of fatigue can be due to weakness or overwork, poor nourishment and bad food habits, mental tension, etc. Excessive fatigue turns into exhaustion and becomes the cause of numerous ailments. In Ayurveda this state is called *dhatukashya*, which means the destruction of body's reserves. Americans like to call the state of exhaustion as 'burn out'. People in today's world like to push themselves to their uttermost limit, as modern civilisation is mind-oriented. They do not go by the feeling that 'I cannot take it any more and I need to rest'. They follow an obsessive-compulsive behaviour pattern: 'I have no choice, I must do it'. When we exhaust our bodies to such a limit, all functions are affected, in particular our nerves and brain.

Risk factor 8

High blood pressure or hypertension

"Hypertension or high blood pressure is a symptom and not a disease by itself. It is important that you learn to find out why the blood in the streams of your inner being is running more rapidly than usual and learn to stop the causes of turbulence in these streams. Hypertension or high pressure of blood (HBP) flowing in your smooth arteries destroys the fine infrastructure of the blood canals, affect their flexibility (hardens them) and can bring you at the brink of cardiovascular disorders, paralysis, stroke and other countless disorders."

This is a citation from my own book on hypertension, which is not yet published. Hypertension is a risk factor that leads to many disorders, but is itself caused by the risk factors described here.

For healthy cerebral blood supply, one needs right density and pressure of blood. The blood supply to the brain is through the blood-brain barriers and not through arteries. It is a very delicate system and if the blood is too dense or does not have an appropriate pressure, the brain is not properly nourished by blood and its metabolism and functions are affected.

Risk factor 9

Constant mental tension and feeling of helplessness

Tension is a state of mind. Human life has ups and down and a stable person maintains balance in all kinds of situations. To remain under tension and fear or feeling helpless in certain situations gives rise to mental fatigue and exhaustion and affects the mind badly. Some people live perpetually in a state of tension and stress. Small things like a traffic jam or a flight delay is enough to make them feel tense and helpless. This mental phenomenon has unpleasant long-term consequences on mental and physical health.

Risk factor 10

Shocks and traumas

Some life situations and events give us shock and trauma. These affect the human mind and may give rise to delirium which is a precursor of dementia. It is the strength and stability of the mind that help an individual to remain stable in such situations, thus not letting the ill effects of upheavals affect the brain.

Risk factor 11

Dwelling on the past and fearing the future

There are individuals who cling to the past happenings of their lives, either feeling sorry for the difficulties they had to face or regretting the loss of good times. They are generally fearful of the future. This kind of mentality is not good for the mind and has long-term consequences on the mental and physical health of an individual. This attitude gives rise to delirium and hence ultimately to other mental disorders leading to dementia.

Risk factor 12

Hopping thoughts

Some people have a very short attention span and their thoughts digress very fast from one topic to another. At times, this digression is quite out of context. You cannot tell even a short story to such people without interruption and their intervention has no relationship to your story. One word or one incident in your narration may link their thoughts to something completely different and out of context and they quickly interrupt you either by asking a question or telling you something. They repeat that often and they quickly forget the original context of the conversation. It is not the occasional apologetic interruption. It is haphazard thinking and that is why I have named it hopping thoughts. Their thinking process hops from one topic to another and they digress to something quite out of context.

Sometimes, even stable individuals have minor element of hopping thoughts. This happens due to past emotional experiences and associations. We divert our minds from a scene of accident in a movie to our own past experiences and our thoughts are momentarily not within the context of the movie. However, our thoughts quickly revert to the present. In people with unstable mind, the hopping is very superficial and frequent. Their thinking process does not generally return to the original story and such people have also low retention power. If not checked and corrected in time, this becomes a precursor for one of the mental ailments leading to dementia.

I have described here the major risk factors which may lead to dementia or a gradual loss of memory and cognition with aging. The more an individual has of these factors, the more he or she is at risk of getting this disorder. A gradual deformation in the brain takes place leading to the major ailments described earlier. The twelve risk factors described above also apply to other mental ailments. When the living system has hindrances and blockades, the results from diversion from the normal may be varied.

Prevention of the risk factors is the subject of next chapter.

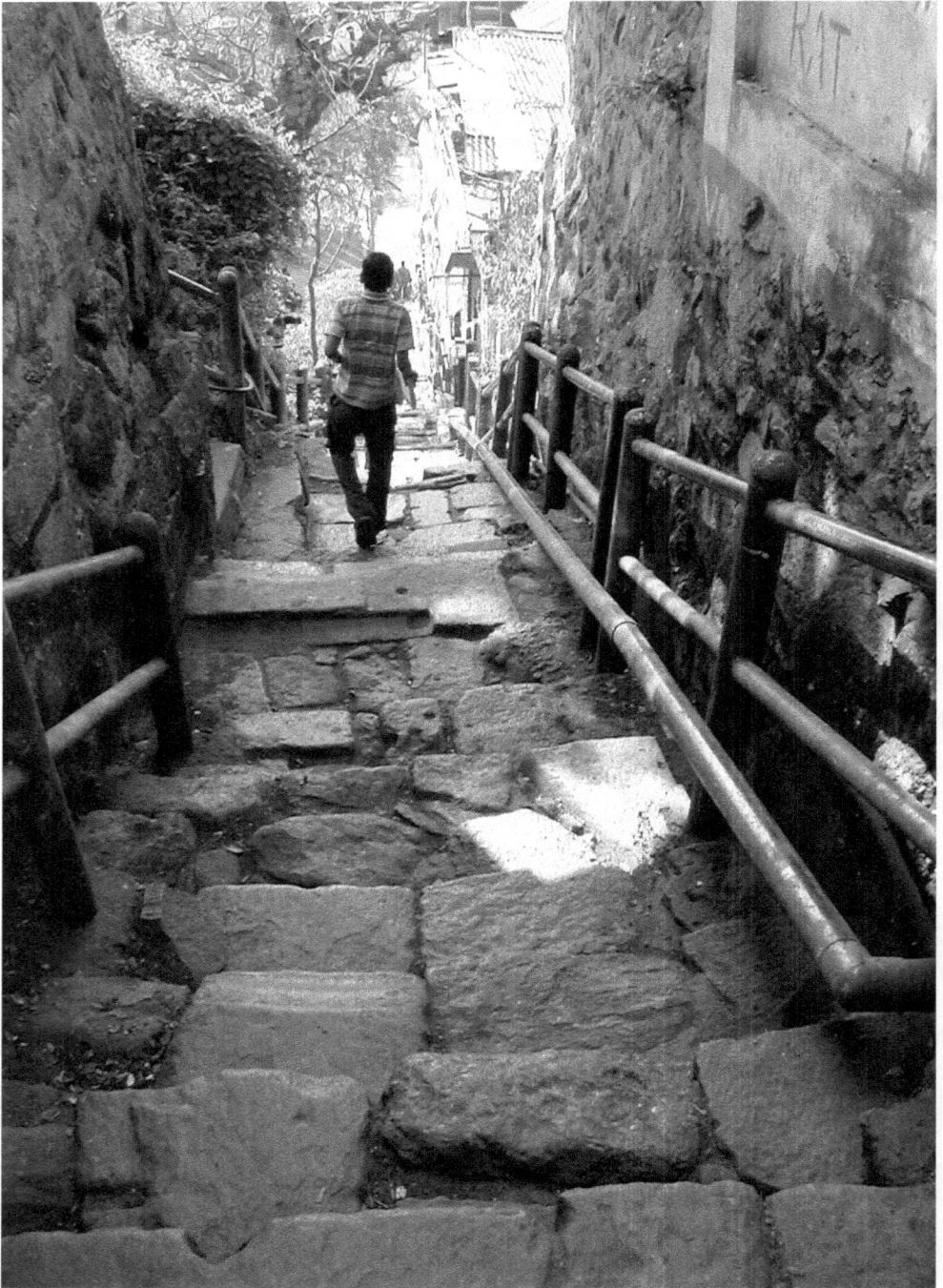

4

Prevention of the Risk Factors

For prevention of dementia, the aim is to protect and preserve nerves, brain and the five senses so that they work in coordination with each other without any deformation until the end of an individual's life. In the present context, this deformation is defined as the loss of retention and inability to recollect the past.

When we talk of prevention on a long-term basis, many questions arise in terms of time. You may say that you are too old for these preventive measures. Others may think that they are still too young and why should they worry about an ailment that may or may not attack them during the later part of their lives. Some others may be sceptical of these measures on the ground that, there is no double blind study possible for these long-term preventive measures. Actually it is never too late or too early to improve the quality of your life. These measures may save you from other ailments as well and provide you more energy besides preventing this particular disorder. Therefore, whether you are 17 or 65, just do it. Correct your posture, let the energy channels flow in your body without hindrances and obstructions and enhance your mental power and physical force. The methods presented here are based upon the age-old Vedic wisdom that has stood the test of time and I do not think they need any approval from modern scientific methods, which are generally non-holistic and reductionist.

Here are the preventive measures for the 12 risk factors stated in the last chapter.

Prevention of Risk Factor 1

Excessive and negative use of the senses

To prevent excessive use of the sense of hearing and its object sound, pay attention to the following:

1. Try to speak as softly as possible. Avoid pointless conversation and be economical in your speech. Remember that words are precious and sound has sanctity. Try not to hear or speak what is unnecessary.

2. Avoid people who speak too much and too loudly. They drain out your energy and leave you with mental fatigue.

3. If your job demands lot of speaking, give your sense of speech and hearing a complete rest after work. Take a hot drink and be in a quiet place for a while.

4. Those of you, who have small children to take care of, should still try to have about 30 minutes of rest between office and home. Go for a quiet walk or take a warm drink.

5. Train your children to speak softly and gently. Lead them to the habit of reading.

6. Avoid unnecessary sounds of radio and television. Switch them off when you are not listening or watching.

7. Listen to some soothing and meditative music in your free time and before going to bed to get rid of the stresses of the day.

8. Change your routine in such a way that, you get some quiet time to yourself everyday, a little more of it every week and may be half a day every month. Every six months take at least a weekend free of sound and worries and go on a retreat. When you read this, it may sound impossible, especially for those who have families with small children. You find time for things you think are important. It is always a question of priorities.

Prevention of risk Factor 2

Incorrect shoulder and neck posture

Correct your posture by keeping your shoulders upright and straight. With a forward bent posture, the cervical vertebrae bulge out and create a circulation problem in the head region, besides pain in neck and shoulders. The following exercise will help you to find out if your shoulder posture is correct.

Lie down and put up your arms as shown in the picture below. If your arms show a curve and are lifted in the middle, you have bent shoulders and a curve in the cervical region. Make an effort to lie down in this posture everyday and try to straighten your arms a little more each time.

The two pictures given below show you an exercise to regularly straighten your shoulders and neck, thus assuring a free flow of energy to the head region. Stand with your hands clasped together and pull them backwards while holding your head straight. After repeating several times, stay in a still position with a backward pull and move left and right in this position as shown in the picture to the right.

Another beneficial yoga posture to straighten the shoulders and neck vertebrae is done in a sitting position. Sit down on the floor cross-legged. In case you cannot sit cross-legged, you can sit on you heels to do this exercise. Those with a stiff body may do this exercise while sitting in a chair. Take your arms back, intertwine the fingers of both your hands and stretch them backwards. Bend your head forwards, while pushing your clasped hands upwards. Some of you may not be able to straighten the arms upwards like shown in the pictures below. But let this not discourage you, as one can acquire flexibility with regular practice.

Sitting cross-legged   Sitting on heels

If you have no neck or shoulder problem and have pain in the lower back, this should be also treated. The vertebral column is made of 33 vertebrae, which are connected to each other with a fine disc like beads in a necklace. In fact, pain in the lower back, if related to the backbone may also spread to the upper region. Since a large number of people of all ages suffer from back pain, I suggest that you do the following six exercises which are meant for the entire backbone.

Prishtavansh asanas or the backbone exercises[*]

Exercise 1

Lie down on your back and put your hands slightly apart from the body and join your feet. Turn your feet in one direction and head in the other. Make the movements slowly and simultaneously, while you inhale. Stay in this position for some seconds while holding the breath. Return to the straight posture slowly and smoothly while exhaling.

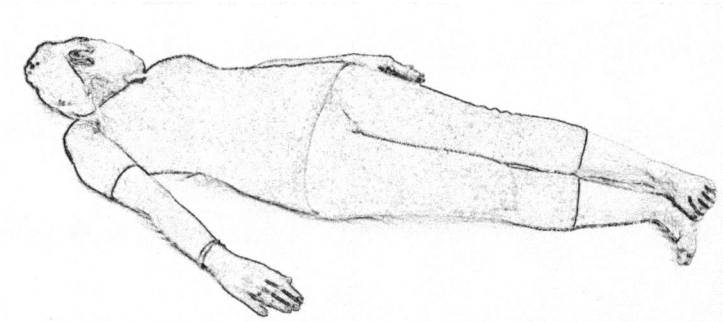

Stay in the straight posture for a duration of few breaths and repeat the same in the opposite direction. This is one cycle and repeat this ten times.

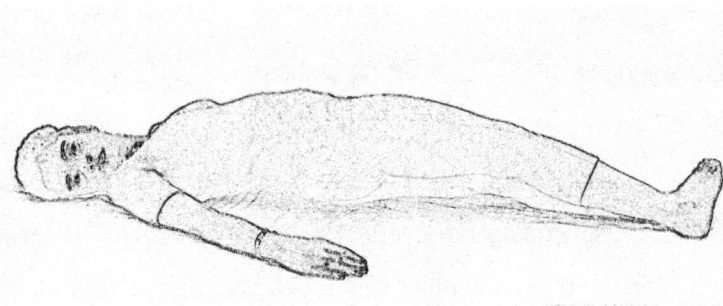

---

[*] I have been teaching these exercise since my student days from eighties and have benefited millions of people around the world. They were also written in my first yoga book published in 1988. The latest edition of this book *Yoga: A Natural Way of Being* is available at www.amazon.com.

Exercise 2

Lie down on your back straight as you have done for the previous exercise, but put your right feet over the left as shown in the picture below. Turn

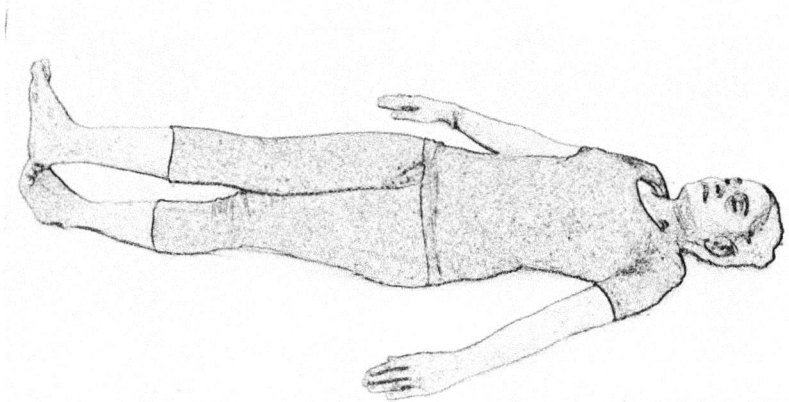

slowly the head on one side while turning your feet in the opposite direction. Inhale while making this movement, hold the breath while in this posture and exhale while coming back to the straight position.

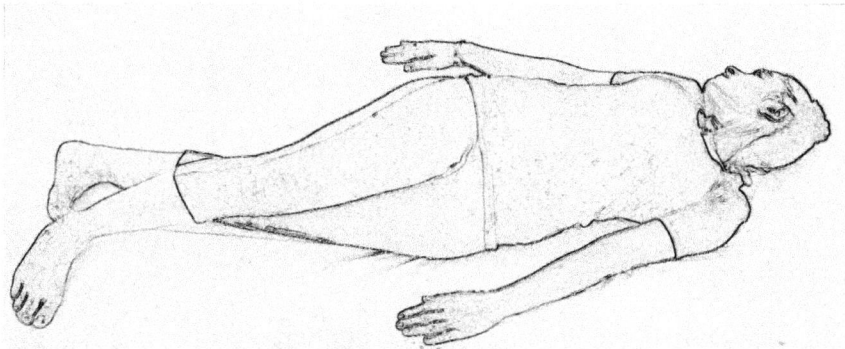

Repeat the same for the opposite direction. Do the exercise ten times.

There is a second part of this exercise, which you do by putting the left foot over the right.

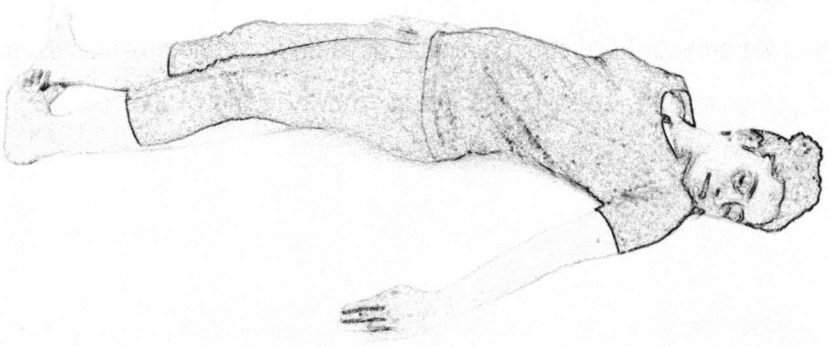

Exercise 3

This exercise is done with your legs folded and your feet on the ground as shown in the figure below.

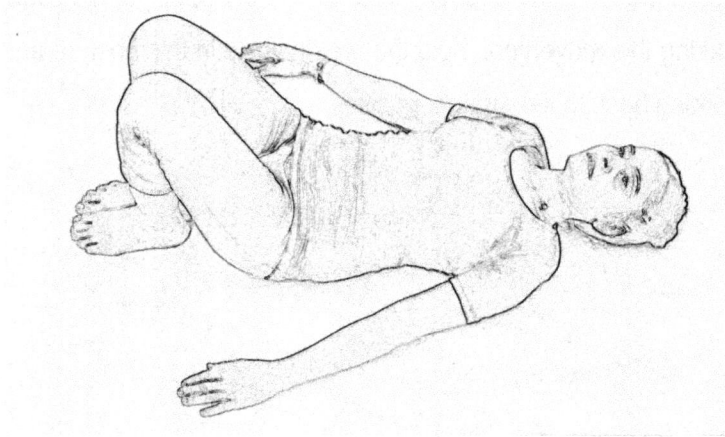

As you have done in the earlier exercises, turn your head in one direction while you turn your feet in the opposite direction. Make sure that you do the movement slowly while inhaling.

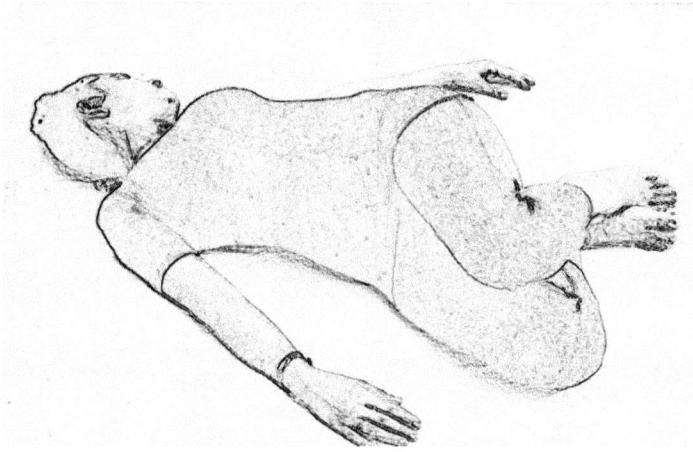

Repeat the same for the opposite direction. Do this exercise about ten times.

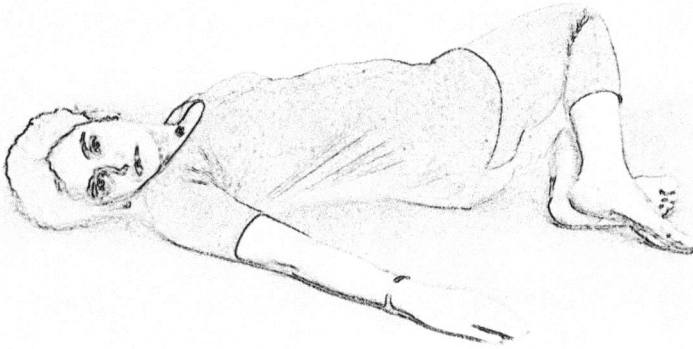

Exercises 4-6

These three positions are essentially the same as the previous three, but they are done while you lie on your stomach. In this posture, while you are turning your head and the legs, they are not in the opposite directions but in the same direction. Given below are the three pictures that depict these three exercises. Repeat each several times as you have done earlier.

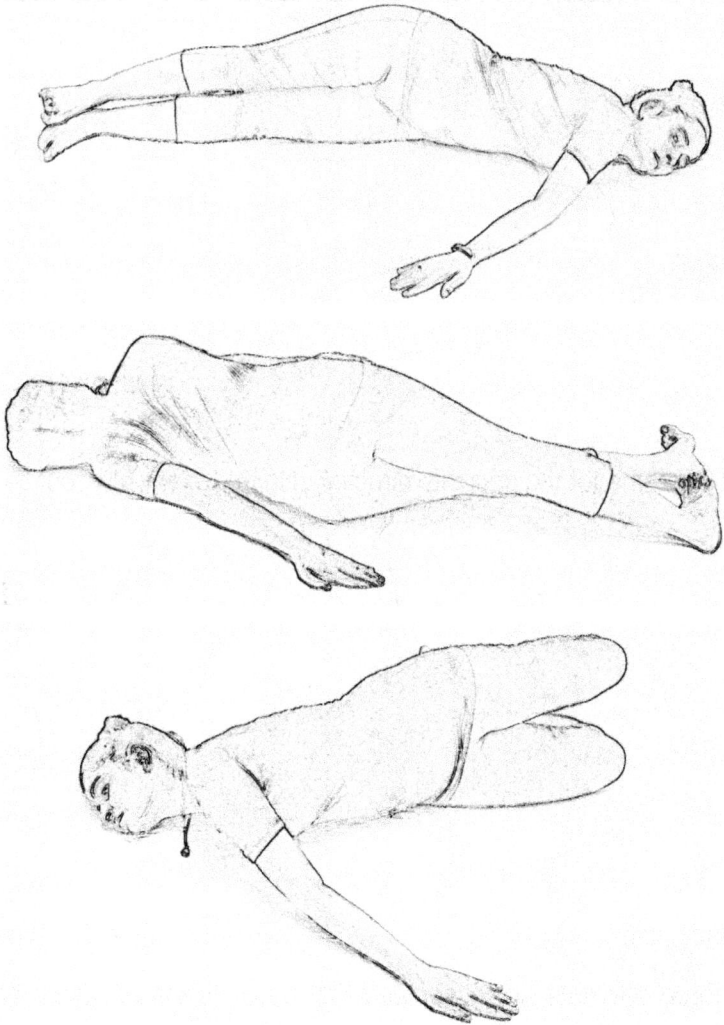

Prevention of risk Factor 3

Incorrect Breathing

Deep and conscious breathing is essential for a good physical and mental health. As explained in the last chapter, the air we inhale is the living element of the cosmos and our system should properly inhale and assimilate it. Improper breathing affects your whole body, as with each breath, we replenish our body with five elements. Space or ether is one element, which is a prerequisite to any existence. With each breath, we inhale both ether and air. The third element is fire, and we take it inside us in the form of heat of the atmosphere. Imagine yourself always breathing in the air that is kept at below zero or above 50°C. Even the thought of it is unpleasant. Thus, the equilibrium of the fire element in the air we inhale is essential. The fourth fundamental element is water and we all know that the inhalation of the absolutely dry air will cause haemorrhage in our nasal passage and may also lead to other severe health complications. The water element is essential and is always there in the air we inhale.

A large part of the air is made of nitrogen, which makes the substantial part of our body in the form of proteins. There are many other elements of earth (carbon, silicon, calcium, phosphorus, etc.) in the air. The vital quality of the air changes with time of the day, weather, climate and geographical location, and that affects directly our lives. We must remember that the intake of vital air lasts until we are alive and that is why the sages called it *prana* or the living element. By regulating our breath and controlling its journey into our being, we, therefore, control our cosmic interaction with our mental and physical processes and learn to influence them with the cosmic energy. Exhaling the air is also a means of detoxifying our body.

For training in right way of breathing, it is suggested that you learn to practice *pranayama*. From the eight parts of yoga, one is *pranayama* or the controlled and organised breathing. The literal meaning of *pranayama* is to develop control over one's *prana*.

Initiation into *pranayama*

There are three parts of the pranayama—the inhalation, exhalation and the absence of these two. Not inhaling and exhaling properly and with appropriate pauses may affect your power of retention; you may get headaches, throat or other respiratory tract infection, it may affect your senses and you may get easily fatigued. Therefore, practice and repeatedly check yourself to breathe in an appropriate yogic manner. Devote five minutes in the morning and five in the evening to do these simple four steps in fresh air or with an open window.

Step 1: Sit down cross-legged or in another posture in a relaxed manner. Begin to inhale in a regular but gradual manner until nearly to your total capacity. Keep your entire concentration on the *prana*, its rhythm and follow its journey inside you. Relax and keep the air in, as long as you can and then exhale gradually with the same rhythm. Let your concentration not divert from your breath. When you have exhaled completely, stay without air a little and concentrate on your inner space. Repeat this whole process several times and gradually increase the timings of inhalation and exhalation as well as of holding with air and without it.

Step 2: This step involves energising two sides of the body separately. The left and right sides of the body represent *tamas* and *rajas* respectively. They can also be compared to moon (left) and sun (right). This practice is done by closing one nostril and breathing exclusively with the other like described above for all the four parts of the *pranayama*. Pick up your right hand and close your right nostril with your thumb and inhale through your left nostril. Hold the air inside by closing also your left nostril with your ring finger (See figures below). Lift your ring finger and exhale from the left side and replace the ring finger again to hold the lungs without air. Repeat the procedure six to ten times exclusively with left nostril. Later, repeat the same for the right nostril while you keep your left nostril closed. This is called *nadishodhan* or purification of channels. You have purified left and right channels with this practice.*

Step 3: In this step, you inhale through one nostril and exhale through the other and for the following round; you inhale through the nostril through which you have previously exhaled. Begin inhaling through the right nostril while the left is closed with your thumb. Then close also the right nostril with

---

* There are three principal energy channels in the body located at left and right of the vertebral column and in the centre. They intertwine with each other and cross each other at seven different places. Their crossing is the site for seven major energy chakras of the subtle body or the energy body. For more details of this theme, see my book: *Yoga: A Natural Way of Being.* It is available at www.amazon.com.

your ring finger to hold the air inside. Let the air out through the left nostril by lifting the thumb and continue to keep the ring finger on the right nostril. Close also the left nostril now to keep the lungs without air. For the next breath, inhale through the left nostril and continue the procedure. Repeat this six to ten times. This purifies the central channel of the body.

Step 4: In this step, you do the inhalation through both the nostrils but close them with your thumb and ring finger when you have inhaled and when you are holding the lungs without air. This step will help you to prolong the timings of the four steps of *pranayama*.

Prevention of risk Factor 4
Nasal Blockades

Free the nasal passage from phlegm blockades or polyps. Some people have perpetually blocked nasal passages and that sows seeds for diverse mental ailments. They cannot breathe properly or do pranayama practices due to that. Here are few steps to keep the nasal passage healthy and free from dirt and infections.

1. After taking a hot shower, dip your two fingers in mustard oil, put them into your nostrils and inhale. This may make you sneeze. Blow your nose strongly after this practice.

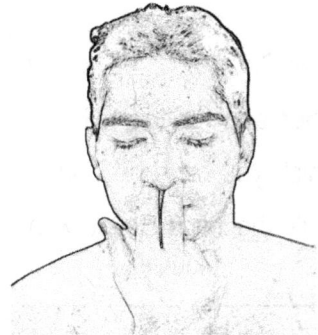

2. Make it a habit to blow your nose strongly after a hot shower to take out the accumulated mucous in the nasal passage. In a dry season or living in heated houses, the nasal passages get dry and in some

cases irritation is felt. Smear the nasal passages with a finger dipped in ghee (clarified butter) several times a day, especially before going to bed.

3. *Jal neti* is a yogic practice for cleaning the nasal passages with water. For doing this practice, you need a small pot with a nozzle called *neti* pot. Fill it with potable lukewarm water. Hold the pot in your right hand. Tilt your head slightly backward, then on the left side, and then slightly forward. Relax in this position, open your mouth and breathe freely from it. Insert the nozzle of the pot in your right nostril and tilt it softly. Let the water enter through right nostril and come out through the left. Let the water flow smoothly by continuous tilting until the pot is empty. Blow your nose after this practice in order to clear the passages. Now repeat the same from left to right nostril. *Jal neti* activates the mucous-secreting cells of the nasal passage and that is why you may have a momentary feeling of having a slight cold. The epithelial cells of the mucous membrane of the nasal passage are activated by *jal neti* and this practice keeps them active to fight any attack of virus, bacteria, or polluted air. After *jal neti*, some of you may experience that your sense of smell has been very much enhanced. The process of cleaning the nasal passages with water activates also the sensory cells, and one becomes capable of smelling nearly undetectable odours as well as odours from the internal parts of one's body.

Caution: It is advised that this practice should be learned with a teacher. If the position of the head is not accurate in order to allow the gravitational flow of water from one passage to another, there is a danger of water entering in the windpipe. This may cause an obstruction in breathing and coughing.

4. Another important step to free the nasal passage is vapour inhalation with some drops of a mixture of etheric oil in it. The details of this method are described in the next step.

5. Some people are not conscious that their nasal passages are partially blocked. They should do some rapid breathing several times a day through nose to make sure that the passages are open.

Prevention of risk Factor 5

Chronic cold, excessive mucous in head region and sinusitis[*]

There is no better method to cure and prevent chronic cold and sinusitis than to do *jalneti* (see above) daily. This practice slowly opens the blocked

---

[*] This is cited from my book *Ayurveda: A way of Life,* Chapter 9. The latest edition of this book is available at www.amazon.com

passages and reduces pain due to accumulation of mucous in the sinus. Use warm water for *jalneti*. It helps melt cumulative mucous and brings it out. *Kapha* from the nasal passage comes out with *jalneti* and it frees the passage for *vāta* and helps soften the accumulated *kapha* in the inner parts, like around the eyes and in the upper parts of the cheeks. You will observe that when you are doing *jalneti* regularly, old, dark-coloured phlegm may come out for the first few days. However, after several days, only a fluid will come out, and the pain due to sinusitis will disappear.

If your nostrils are dry, warm water may hurt them. Smear some ghee in the nostrils prior to *neti* and should also do *neti* with pure natural milk mixed 50% with water from time to time.

The second part of the cure for sinusitis is steam inhalation with a mixture of etheric oils in it. The inhalation is done with special breathing exercises as described below. Either use a commercial mixture of etheric oils or add a little bit of pain-relieving balm in boiling hot water. You may also make your own mixture for inhalation with the following ingredients:

Eucalyptus oil	50 gm
Citronella	50 gm
Menthol crystals	50 gm
Fennel oil	20 gm
Camphor	20 gm
Lavender oil	10 gm

Mix them together and let the mixture stand for at least a week before use. Shake the bottle three to four times a day for about 10 minutes each. This

mixture can be preserved for years if kept in a tightly closed dark bottle in a cool place. Never use plastic bottles to keep these oils. Always replace the lid immediately otherwise they evaporate. Take some from the stock for everyday use.

To get rid of sinusitis, you should do inhalations regularly by adding a few drops of the above mixture in boiling hot water. Take a steam inhalation apparatus (called generally Face Sauna) or let the water boil at a low heat in a small pot. Add few drops of the oil mixture and begin inhalation by simply breathing in these vapours and let them go inside whatever way possible— nose or mouth. This will give an initial help to open the passage. To open the blocked nasal passage, take a deep breath from the vapours through your mouth and try to exhale through your nose. In this process, slowly, the nasal passage will be freed from phlegm.

At each step of inhalation, add two to three drops of the oil. For the next step, inhale rhythmically through your mouth and exhale through your nose. Then inhale through your nose and exhale through your mouth. In this process, you might have to stop in between to blow your nose and spit out excessive saliva. This inhalation activates the salivary glands. Blow your nose with force so that the old stuck phlegm is blown out. After this, inhale from one nostril while the other is kept closed (as you did for *pranayama*). Keep the vapours inside by closing both nostrils. Then exhale from the other nostril and inhale from the same. Repeat this a few times so that the passage between your two nostrils gets free, and by closing both nostrils, the vapours are forced to go to the other parts of the sinus.

The next step is to inhale to your full capacity through nostrils or mouth and then hold the nostrils, shut the mouth and try to push the air out with pressure. Since mouth and nostrils are kept closed, the vapours will be forced to go to the other parts because of the pressure you are applying. You may feel some sensation in your ears by doing so.

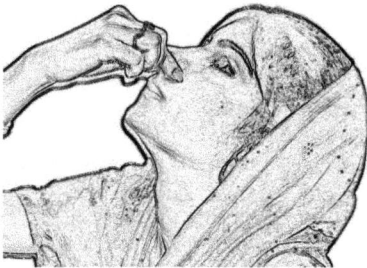

Lastly, inhale vapours to your full capacity, close your mouth and nose as you did above and bend backwards. While in this position, tilt your head sideways. Repeat this several times. Like this, the medicated vapours can reach different parts of your head.

The vapours with etheric oils have a high penetration capacity. They are capable of softening the blocked mucous in the sinus passages and take it out. They can also cure the infection by making an extremely disagreeable environment for the virus and bacteria, as some of the etheric oils in the above mixture have anti-viral, anti-fungus and antibiotic qualities. However, to get rid of the infection completely, you will have to do this practice regularly because these viruses and bacteria multiply very quickly. After the inhalation, lie down for some time and keep yourself warm.

For completely eradicating the sinus problem, you should also take a treatment with germinated wheat, which is described in Chapter 8.

Prevention of risk Factor 6

A chronic imbalance of body's air and space energy— vata

This is one of the major risk factors leading to dementia and every effort should be made to keep its equilibrium for preventing dementia. I have given a chart below about vata from my book *Ayurveda: A Way of Life* to make you understand the effect of the imbalance of vata, factor causing it and methods of treatment.

Our modern way of living is vata oriented and we need to pay special attention to keep our equilibrium due to a hectic pace of life. Please read carefully the factors which lead to this imbalance and take immediate steps for regaining equilibrium. Warm drinks, warm and unctuous meals, oil application on the body followed by a hot bath or steam bath are some of the simple measures one can take. You also need a peaceful atmosphere and rest to balance the vata energy in your body.

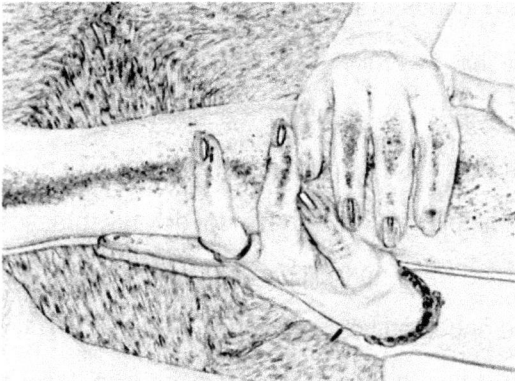

Vata is dry and cold by nature, and that is why wet and unctuous measures are suggested. A continuous imbalance of vata is very bad for the nerves. The thinking process begins to work in a hectic manner. One is distracted easily and is unable to concentrate. One becomes nervous and unstable. If you get such symptoms, suspend your activities for a few days and saturate your body with oil by rubbing warm oil on it. Oil your scalp also (see champi in the next chapter) and sit in a hot bath. After the bath, wrap your body in a bathrobe and go to a warm bed (prepared beforehand with a hot water bottle) and sleep for some time.

Given below are some principal factors that you can immediately put to use for healing vata imbalance.

1. Keep warm and avoid exposure to air even in summer.

2. Do not take cold drinks. Drink warm water, previously boiled with cardamom.

3. Oil saturation of the body and the scalp is the key feature to cure vata imbalance.

4. A steam bath or simply a hot bath after oil saturation followed by an appropriate rest provides great relief.

5. Take teas with ginger, cardamom, basil, pepper, fennel, coriander, and liquorice. If you do not have the knowledge of all these, take them in dried form in equal quantity and grind them. Your pharmacist can do that for you. Boil half teaspoon of this in half litre water and take it is a tea.

6. Make a simple spice mixture with the following five products in equal quantity: cumin, ajwain (an Indian spice like thyme), *Nigella sattiva* (named *kalonji* in Indian shops abroad), fenugreek seeds and cress seeds. Grind them and mix them well. Take half a teaspoon of this in the morning and half in the evening. Put this powder in your mouth and swallow it with some warm water. Take it for at least 15 days.

7. Take always warm meals accompanied by soups. Eat punctually, 2/3 stomach full and no snacks between meals. Never eat before

the previous meal is digested.

Vata imbalance and healing measures

Vata-dominating persons	Factors that cause vata imbalance	Signs of vata imbalance	Treatment of vata imbalance
• Agile • Quick and unrestricted in their movements; • Swift in action; • Quick in fear and other emotions; • Get easily irritated; • Intolerant to cold and shiver easily; • Coarse hairs and nails; • Prominent blood vessels	• Fasting; • Excessive physical exercise; • Exposure to cold; • Laziness; • Staying awake late at night; • Windy weather; • Old age; • Evening and last part of the night; • Over-ripened or stale foods; • Injury; • Blood loss; • Excessive sexual intercourse; • Uneven posture; • Suppression of natural urges; • Anxiety; • Guilt.	• Stiffness and pain in the body; • Bad taste and dryness in the mouth; • Lack of appetite; • Stomach-ache; • Dry skin; • Fatigue; • Dark coloured stool; • Insomnia; • Pain in temporal region; • Giddiness; • Tremors; • Yawning; • Hiccups; • Malaise; • Delirium; • Dull complexion; • Withdrawn and timid behaviour	• Food dominant in sweet and sour rasas; • Hot therapeutic measures • Enemas; • Massages; • Anointing; • Appropriate rest, relaxation and sleep; • Peaceful atmosphere; • Cheerful mental state; • Treatment with diet and drug

8. Keep your system clean and if you have constipation, treat it immediately. Take a hot glass of milk before going to bed. Drink hot water in the morning and do exercises. Eat plenty of vegetables and fruits and take unctuous food. Treat constipation by changing your way of living rather than taking purgatives.

Prevention of risk factor 7

General body weakness, frequent bouts of fatigue and exhaustion

As you see in the above table, fatigue is one of the features of vata imbalance. Fatigue also occurs with improper nutrition, lack of assimilation of nutrients and too much physical labour without appropriate rest. One should learn to accept fatigue, eat properly and take appropriate rest. Besides that, one needs to take rasayanas or rejuvenating products to build up body's immunity and vitality. Some recipes to this effect have been described in the last chapter of this book.

Fatigue has to be dealt with regularly and not accumulated to exhaustion level or the burnout, as the Americans like to call it. It is recommended in Ayurveda to perform six monthly cleansing practices and than take rasayana to enhance immunity and vitality. For more details on this theme and Ayurvedic lifestyle, refer to my book *Programming Your Life with Ayurveda*. It is a practical Manual.

Prevention of risk factor 8

High blood pressure (Hypertension)

I have already stated that the high blood pressure or hypertension is due to some blockades in the body. Low blood pressure is usually due to weakness and fatigue. Both low and high blood pressure may be the side-effect of some allopathic medications. Make every effort to keep your blood pressure under control and do not jump to take regular allopathic drugs on the slightest rise in your blood pressure. Use alternative methods and diet control first to stabilise your blood pressure. I give below some principal precautions and measures to be taken. However, this theme is going to be the subject of another book.

1. Take rest, proper and timely diets and liquid food. Fresh pressed fruit juice from carrots, apple, pomegranate, beetroot, orange, etc. is recommended. Take several fruits along with large portion of carrots so that the juice is not sour. The fresh pressed juice should be consumed within half an hour after pressing, otherwise it causes vata imbalance.

2. If you are a healthy person and have mild hypertension, which is not due to another disorder, try to cure it with lifestyle changes, diet and mild medicine. After an oil saturation massage and hot bath, take a mild purgation like senna leaves or something similar the next day before going to bed. After this treatment, stay on very simple vegetarian diet cooked with rejuvenating and balancing spices like cardamom, cumin, fennel, ajwain or thyme, etc. and eat in a moderate quantity.

3. Take fruits like bananas, papayas, pears, dates, sweat apples and raisins. Avoid sour fruits. Take appropriate rest and lead a disciplined life with regular hours of sleep.

4. Along with the careful lifestyle, there are homeopathic products available to regulate hypertension. Hypertensin has been a

wonderful German medication for this but unfortunately is not available any more for the reasons unknown to me. Diacard is another German medication for hypertension. A good pharmacist can help you chose a homeopathic product for regulating your hypertension. I repeat again that these recommendations are meant for the mild cases and not the extreme cases, because the latter are generally the symptoms of another disorder in the body.

Prevention of risk factor 9

Frequently facing mental tension and feeling of helplessness

Tension and helplessness are the states of mind created by you. You need to learn methods to strengthen your mind. Dhyana or the yogic concentration exercises should be done regularly for few minutes everyday in the morning upon getting up and in the evening before going to bed.

Initiation in Dhyana

Do regularly the breathing exercises described earlier for several months.

After your breath flow becomes smooth and effortless, do the breathing exercises by sending your breath to the navel point with all your concentration at that point. Put the four fingers and thumb of your right hand together and put that on the navel as shown in the figure below.

Do this practice in the morning and in the evening regularly, even for five minutes

69

only. When you get an unbroken concentration on the navel point, you should be able to do this practice without putting your fingers at this point. Being regular is the key feature, as the progress in *dhyana* is very gradual.

Just as you brush your teeth two times every day, with same regularity you should make *dhyana* practice your way of life. The inner wisdom will awaken in you, you will develop intuitive power and your mind will become strong enough to face the ups and downs of life.

Prevention of risk factor 10

Shocks and traumas

We face shocks and traumas because we have to deal with unexpected situation. What can be a bigger shock for parents than to lose their young child or for young children to lose their mother or father? Disease, accident and natural calamities are some other reasons for shocks and traumas. We must develop the attitude to accept that life is ever changing and anything unexpected can happen any time. When it happens to others, think that it can also happen to you also. Do not feel shattered with events in life. Think of doing your best in a given situation. Our present life is the result of our previous karma. On the results of karma already done, we have no control. But for our present karma, we have control and can train ourselves to be mentally stable and strong so that the ill effects of the past karma is minimised and we sow better seeds for future. Inculcate this wisdom also in your children. The practice of *dhyana* described above can help you acquire this wisdom in a natural manner.

Prevention of risk factor 11

Dwelling in the past and fearing the future

Do not dwell upon your past negative experiences and do not ask why they happened. Also do not regret the loss of positive experiences or good times in your life. Eliminate the presence of the past by developing inner stillness (sattva) and learn to live in the moment. What was is already gone and you cannot bring it back. The present time is in your hands and you can devote your energy and goodwill to make the best possible use out of it and to invest in your future in terms of good health and a strong mind. Worrying about the future is as useless as trying to count the stars or the hairs on one's head. Nobody can predict the future. Some people run to different astrologers to know about the future. Good astrologers can tell you about the results of karma and the good and bad periods of life. But they cannot predict the future, as the future is the result of a combination of your present and past karma. For example, something positive or negative happens in your life due to your past karma. The manner you deal with it by your present karma can be constructive or destructive in the context of that happening. You perform your present karma with your power of discretion or buddhi. Nobody can predict your present karma and that is where your freedom lies. That stops life from being determined. In my opinion, that is the beauty of life, that we do not know the next moment. Learn to remain in a relaxed state and train yourself to live in the present moment. Do not sow the seeds for an ailment by dwelling on the past or worrying about the future.

Prevention of risk factor 12

Hopping thoughts

This state of mind happens due to excess of rajas in life and imbalance of vata. They are both interconnected. Too much rajas give rise to vata imbalance, whereas vata imbalance gives rise to a hectic state of mind. For example, vata imbalance causes constipation and if constipation remains unattended, it gives rise to a restless mind and bad dreams. It also leads to lack of concentration of the mind. In such a subject, treating the constipation gives rise to a feeling of liberation in both body and mind. Constipation ruins the inner climate of the body, and nerves are very sensitive to smell and each odour has its negative or positive effect.

Pranayama, yogic exercises and postures, oil treatments like champi or head massage, *shirodhara* or *shirobasti*, quiet atmosphere and repetition of a mantra (japa) are some of the things that help get rid of hopping thoughts and give the mind the ability to concentrate. Please follow the instruction for japa given in Chapter 6.

5

Getting rid of the Fear of Dementia

Dementia has been a much talked about subject in the European media during the last three years. However, the public has little understanding of the disease and its fundamental causes. Repeated discussion about the disease and its rapid spread has induced tremendous fear in public. After having forgotten something or not being able to recall some event immediately, people tend to joke about it by saying- Oh, I am getting dementia! Or they tell each other the same thing. Evidently, it is the fear speaking in them. I would like to advise you that one should never pronounce the name of such a deadly disorder even jokingly. In the Vedic tradition, we believe in the power of the sound in the form of mantras and their repetition and therefore it is always recommended never to utter evil and unwanted words.

Please pay attention to the following information about dementia to get rid of your fear:

1. Forgetting a few things here and there is normal for human beings and is not a sign of dementia. This forgetfulness is due to fatigue, exhaustion, fear or excessive pressure of work. Instead of imagining that it is dementia, take appropriate rest and diet and be in a calm and peaceful atmosphere.

2. For curing a temporary phase of forgetfulness, *champi* (head massage) and body oil saturation massage followed by a hot bath is

73

very helpful. Dip your fingers in oil (sesame, coconut, olive oil or any medicated preparation) and rub your scalp vigorously. Massage from all sides until the scalp is completely saturated with oil. Make your strokes stronger and faster and in all directions of the scalp. Rest for a short while after the head massage.

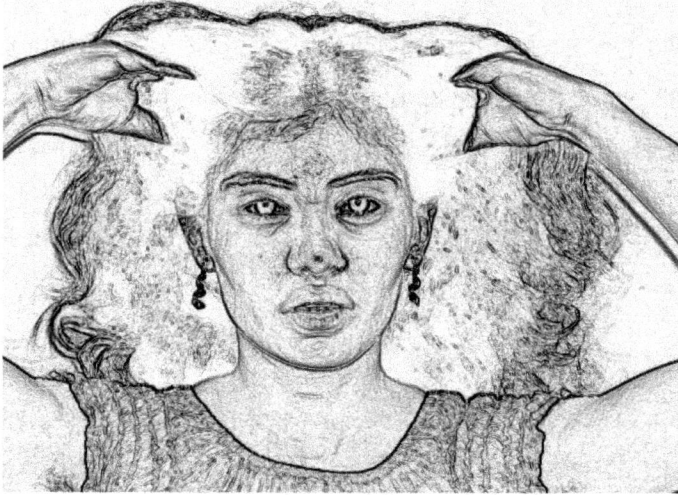

3. The pressure points for brain and nerves are on thumb and big toe. Massage these with oil by applying pressure at the root of the thumb and the big toe. Massage also the entire hands and feet with oil and then soak them in hot water for about ten minutes.

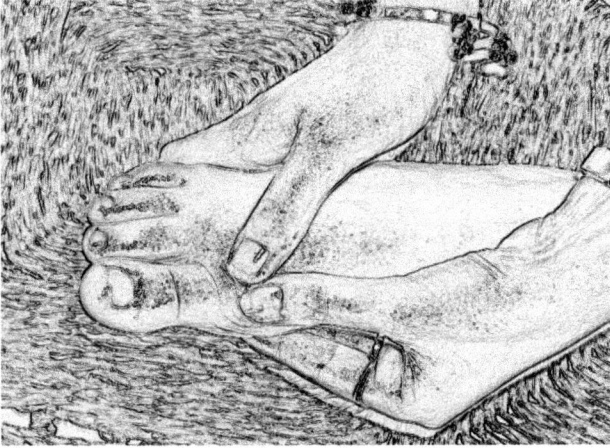

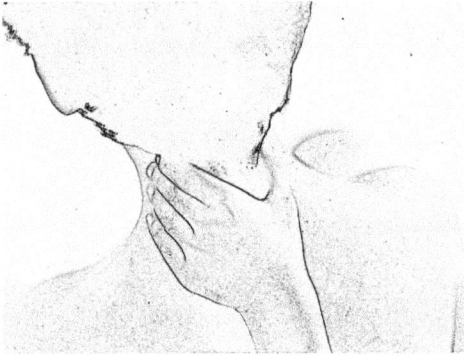

4. Do a shoulder and neck massage and pay attention to the neck exercises shown in the previous chapter. Press the points shown in the picture to relieve and relax the nerves and the blood vessels.

5. Oil massage on temporal regions and ears and pressing all parts of the ear lobe helps alleviate mental fatigue and revives the mental power.

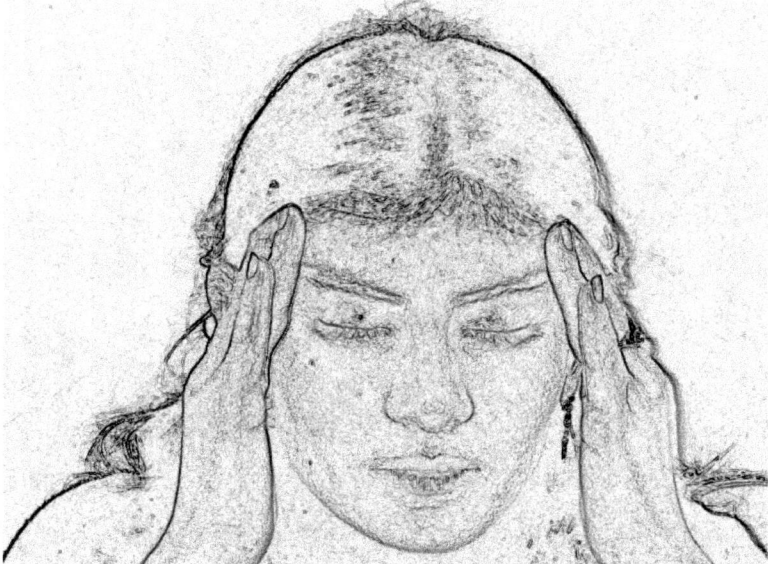

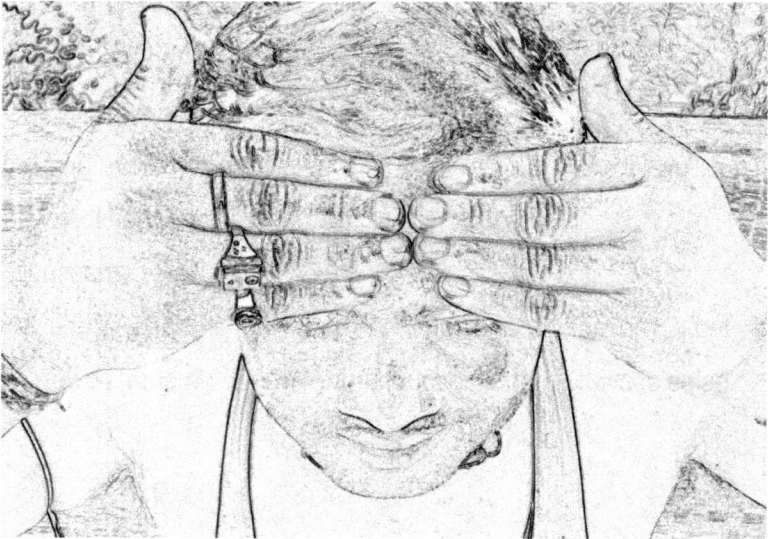

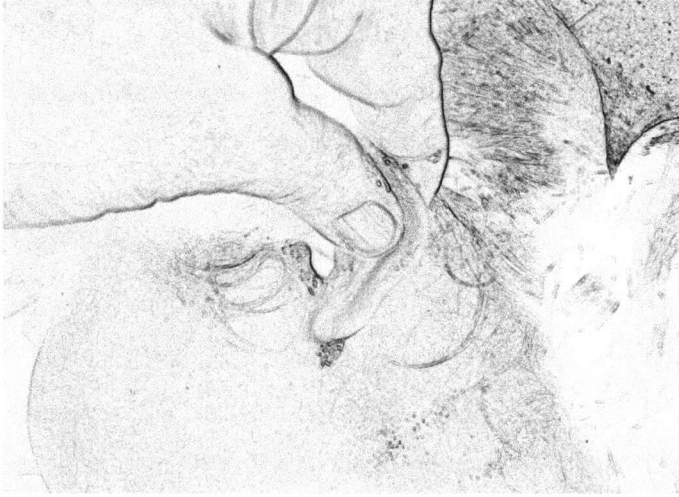

6. Take a resolve that you are going to invest enough in your health to remain healthy and wise until the end of your life and not become sick and senile.

7. Whenever you happen to meet a person suffering from dementia or watch or read a report about the rapid spread of dementia, make a resolution that you are not going to be a victim and that you will take all the measures and use your will to prevent it and keep your mind healthy and cheerful until the end of your life. If you feel disturbed, do some rapid pranayama like dhaukani or kapalbhati to dissipate the fear in you (see the boxes below for details). These are the advanced pranayama, which can be done if you have been regularly doing the previously described basic pranayama. Without that preparation, these practices can be exhausting and may do harm in certain cases.

Dhaukani pranayama[*]

Dhaukani means bellows. It is an instrument which is used to blow air with pressure on the fire. This breathing practice comprises of pushing out the air with force and in a gush. In this breathing practice, you are going to imitate the function of the bellows with your breathing.

Sit cross-legged or in a chair. Inhale small amount of air and simultaneously pull inwards your abdomen muscles as far as you can. Blow out the air with force and while doing so, your abdomen muscles will be released back to normal position. Do not move your shoulders or other parts of your body in this process. Repeat this for several days until you can do this effortlessly.

Caution: Do not do this practice until three hours after having eaten.

Kapalabhati pranayama

Kapalabhati is a pranayama practice that involves inhaling towards the head region in a rapid manner.

Sit down in a comfortable manner, preferably cross-legged. Start breathing in a manner as if you are pulling your breath upwards to your head. Kapalbhati involves breathing rapidly and sending the prana energy to the head region. Pull up the air with great force and push it out with the similar force. Repeat this according to your capacity. In case you have problems, do it by giving some pauses of normal breathing in-between.

---

[*] *Caution: This practice should not be done by persons who have asthma or any other respiratory trouble or by those who are weak, feeble or anaemic.*

6

Yogic Methods to Fight Senility

According to the Yoga Guru Patanjali, there are five kinds of modifications of the mind (characteristic qualities of the flow of thoughts). These are either afflictive (*klesha*) or non-afflictive (*aklesha*). These modifications are i) evidence, ii) misconception, iii) fancy, iv) sleep and v) memory. (see Chapter 2 for details of the modifications).They may be painful or not. In fact, whether they bring us pain or pleasure in the worldly sense, they will come under the category of afflictive. Material and sensuous pleasures do not remain constant in the ever-changing dynamic world. When pleasure departs, there is pain. For a wise person or an adept of yoga, all modifications of the mind are afflictive. In the present context, non-afflictive will be those modifications of the mind, which lead one to wisdom of recognising one's real self, soul as distinct from the destructible and perishable physical self. It is to recognise the impermanence of everything that exists around us including our physical self. The moment we realise that, worldly happenings and events will not agitate us. We will take a balanced view of life and will not be disturbed so easily. With this yogic state of mind, we learn to take life as it comes and will not be affected even by shocks and traumas. Shocks and traumas can cause all kinds of ailments. Here are some case studies of serious disorders due to shock and trauma: i) a woman got paralysis when her husband brought another woman saying that she is too old to have children and he wanted a younger partner to have children; ii) another woman died of a heart attack a year after her husband left her for a younger woman, iii) a middle aged man with his two children studying in the university developed Multiple Sclerosis when he suddenly lost his job, iv) a woman developed dementia due to frontal lobe shrinkage after her husband brought another woman into their house.

Leading a life without expectations and an accepting the 'unexpected' with calmness makes the mind strong and protects from the harmful effects of repression on the brain and nerves. This is perhaps a very different philosophy of life for many of you. It is a training of mind offered in the yogic way of living to keep the mind stable in all kinds of situation. This stability of mind is achieved with constant effort and training. An afflicted state of mind makes one frustrated and unhappy. One becomes a dissatisfied individual and ultimately becomes prey to mental and physical disorders.

We need to learn that life does not move along predictable lines. Anything can happen at anytime. Events in life do not happen at our wish or command. We have to learn to accept the happenings of the world as they unfold. We have to train our mind to attain a sense of contentment. It does not however mean that we should be passive. In yogic thinking, one should put one's best efforts into doing one's duty without anticipation of results. In fact, this state of mind gives one so much mental power that things run smoothly on their own. Once you have attained a sense of contentment and learn to accept reality or the dynamism of life as it unfolds itself, you will remain in a happy mental state. A happy mental state by itself is a healer and of course it prevents ailments. Learn to celebrate each moment of life and try to find something positive in all situations. In truth, the training of mind is lacking in the modern world. These simple things should be taught to children the world over.

AFFLICTED STATE OF MIND

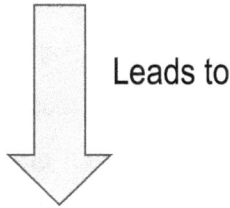

Leads to

DISSATISFACTION

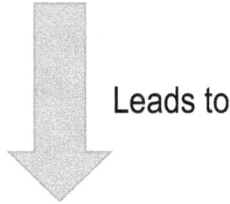

Leads to

UNHAPPINESS

Leads to

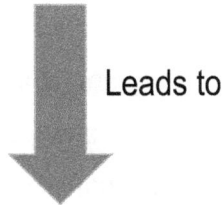

MENTAL AND PHYSICAL DISORDERS

Mental stability can save us from mental disorders. Charaka has defined psychic or mental ailments very beautifully: they are due to unfulfilled desires and facing the undesired. If we have too many desires and wishes, there are chances that many will remain unfulfilled, leading to frustration and thus giving rise to mental disorders. Similarly, we should not continue to live with the undesired. We should either make every effort to get out of the unwanted situation or learn to accept it.

According to the yogic way of thinking, we must train ourselves to look at life as an onlooker. An onlooker is not a spectator. An onlooker is uninvolved in the spectacle of life. Excessive involvement and attachment with worldly happening and goods always lead us to troubled mental state. On the contrary, if we detach ourselves and remain uninvolved with the diverse events and episodes of life, we remain calm and peaceful and attain mental strength. With this philosophy of life, we do not fall prey to mental and physical disorders and certainly not to the disorders leading to dementia.

To strengthen the mind, we need to give it rest and stop its modifications or chain of thoughts with a conscious effort. When we succeed in doing that, we experience a state of yogic bliss (*ananda*). In the Bhagavad Gita, Krishna preached to Arjuna about the importance of yoga and Arjuna gave his opinion on his teaching as follows:

'The yoga which you have described with such facility, I do not see it as practical because of the ever-changing nature of the mind. The mind is very unsteady, turbulent, tenacious and powerful and therefore I consider that restraining it is as unfeasible as controlling the wind'.

In Krishna's response, there were two important words for controlling the mind— repeated practice and detachment. Patanjali has said that the modifications of mind should be hindered by repeated practice and dispassion. For our purpose in the present context, *japa* or the repeated practice of a mantra helps to attain a thought-free mind. It has to be done regularly and with a firm aim in mind.

Japa or the repetition of a mantra*

Choose the smallest mantra called OM and pronounced as au.....m. That ends with a long nasal 'm'. Take a *mala* (rosary) with 108 beads and pronounce this mantra with each bead. Repeat three rosaries in the morning and three in the evening or before going to bed at night. You should do this practice regularly and always with the effort to concentrate on the sound and form of AUM. The sound and form of AUM represent the phenomenon world of colours and forms but all dissolves in one ultimate reality— the *Purusha* or the Universal Soul.

Follow the steps given below for learning the mantra AU.....M.

1. Sit down cross-legged or in another comfortable posture, straighten your back and take a deep breath. Hold the breath for a brief moment and begin to release it gradually. Make sure that the

---

* For more details on this theme, refer to my book: *AUM: the Infinite Energy*, available at www.amazon.com

outflow of the breath is smooth and it is not in a stop-and-go manner. Repeat this for at least five breaths.

2. This step is the same as above, but this time, release your breath with a sound from the deeper part of your throat. This is not yet the sound of AU... we are aiming at. Make sure that your mouth is closed while you do this breathing exercise. Repeat this also for at least five times.

3. Take a deep breath and slowly release it while making the sound of AU...... from the upper part of your throat. In this process, your lips will slightly open and curl. Repeat this also five times.

4. For singing the complete AUM, do the step three and at the end of AU...., gradually transform this tone into a nasal M. The sound of M... should mount towards your head region.

Pranayama

A regular practice of *pranayama* helps prevent ailments. I have already described the four *pranayama* steps for the purification of the energy channels. Integrate them in your daily routine. You need a regular practice of these before you can learn *Kapalbhati* and *Dhaukani pranayama* described in Chapter 5. These two help strengthen and energise the mind. They also help to achieve a thought-free mind and rid you of the mental fatigue. However, you need to repeat them fairly regularly. Otherwise you will feel breathless and will not be able to benefit from them.

7

Strength and Purity of Mind for Dementia prevention

A pure mind is that which is free from the *kleshas* or afflictions. Afflictions are due to the modifications of the mind. To stop afflictions, we have to make an effort to hinder the modifications of the mind, as has been discussed in the previous chapter. In simple words, that implies silencing the mind for brief periods. The mind is constantly fed with new knowledge it obtains through senses along with the previously acquired knowledge in the form of the memory; it is constantly undergoing a chain of thoughts. The senses are partially closed during sleep and the mind is not acquiring new knowledge. However, the previously acquired knowledge in the form of memory is processed even during sleep. The mind never stops. During sleep, it gets partial rest but it only gets real rest by stopping the chain of thoughts and entering into a state of void or nothingness. This is done by withdrawing the senses from the phenomenal world, stopping the chain of thoughts and bringing the mind back to its own pure nature. Purity of mind and strength are simultaneous. How? According to yogic sages, the mind is completely involved with the world through the senses, but when it is brought to silence and void, it immersed in the energy of the soul. Soul is pure energy and the primal cause. By repeated practice and with concentration of the mind, we can achieve this goal of silencing the mind from time to time and invigorate it.

At a higher level than mind is the mati or formulation of ideas with the processed knowledge. At a still higher level is the intellect or buddhi and at the highest level is the soul, which is the cause of being and the real self of an individual. Given below is the figurative form of this analysis of the senses, mind and soul. Existence and functions of body, mind, formulation of ideas and intellect are not possible without the radiations from the energy of soul.

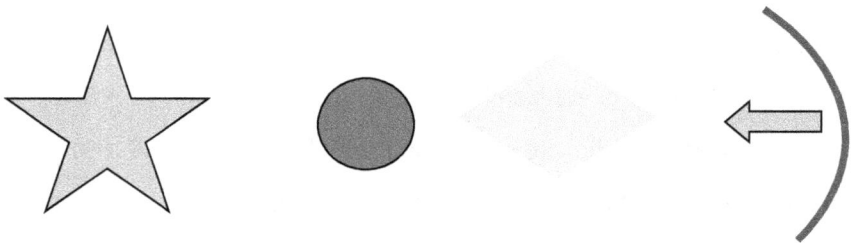

Mind and the five senses   **Mati**   **Buddhi**   **Soul, the cause of being**

The mind in an uninvolved state is in its pure form. It is the state of sattva or stillness. Sattva is a balancing factor of rajas and tamas— the two characteristic qualities of the mind that dominate our day-to-day life. From state of hyper activity during the day, we come to a state of fatigue when body and mind fall into a state of inertia (tamas). We need to incorporate sattva in our actions (rajas) so that we can perform our tasks without oppressing our senses and mind. This oppression at a routine level for a long time becomes the ultimate cause of physical and mental disorders. Charaka stated 2600 years ago the importance of sattva as follows:

The persons having dominating sattva are endowed with memory, devotion, are grateful, learned, pure, courageous, skilful, resolute, fighting in battles with prowess, free from anxiety, having well directed and serious intellect and activities and are engaged in virtuous acts.[*]

The sattva state of mind is not acquired by theoretically learning about stillness and keeping the mind thought-free. It comes with a gradual training of the mind. Given below are some practical suggestions for incorporating in your daily routine for initiating you to lead a sattvic way of life.

1. Upon getting up in the morning, turn towards the east and say a few words of thankfulness to the Sun for giving you another day of life. Seek his blessings so that all your senses work until the end of your life and you may lead a long and fulfilled life.

2. Pay attention when you take a shower or a bath. Make a wish that along with the outer dirt from your body, the inner dirt may also be washed away and may your mind be purified and you achieve inner peace and harmony. In case you have pain, malfunction or any other trouble in any part of your body, concentrate on the flowing water and make a wish that the flowing water may take this disorder away. May this disorder flow down the drain like the dirt from your body.

3. Before eating each meal, take five deep breaths while concentrating on the navel.

---

[*] *Charaka Samhita*, Vimanasthanam, VIII, 110

4. Keep your environment clean and orderly. Do not accumulate unnecessary things. Overly filled work and living spaces give rise to tamasic energy and decrease your mental capabilities. Some people keep all kinds of printed material thinking that they will read them later. Years go by and they gather dust. There are others who accumulate all kinds of stuff related to their hobbies. There are still others who never throw out their old clothes. Accumulated unused stuff gathers the 'dust of time' and this chokes the environment of that individual. Take time to throw away unneeded stuff and keep your environment serene.

5. Before starting your day and going out of the house or starting your car each time, always take a few deep breaths, touch something holy or a pure piece of silver or crystal, etc. Never lose your attention while driving and always take few deep breaths every now and then. Send the *prana* energy to your head region.

6. Take breathing breaks like this throughout the day and send *prana* energy to the different senses and the head every time. It is the matter of two-three breaths every one or two hours and it does not require any extra time.

7. Whenever you have an emotional outburst, do not lose contact with yourself. That means— observe yourself doing that activity. Your whole being should not get involved in that, you should be able to observe yourself getting angry, getting jealous, in a state of self-pity, and so on. That way, you will be able to keep some control on your tamasic thoughts.

8. Before going to bed, bring yourself in harmony with the night's energy and wish for a profound sleep, free of *rajas-* and *tamas*. A state of sleep in which the inner stillness prevails and which is achieved after *pranayama* and *japa* is called *yoganidra*. With *yoganidra*, one can get more rest with fewer hours of sleep.

The seeds of anti-sattva lie in a mental state of discontentment or *asantosha*. Make every effort to attain a contented state of mind (*santosha*). Think of what you have and not what you do not have. With *santosha*, we are able to attain sattva state of mind and can lead a peaceful life. The moment you attain a state of mind of *santosha*, you are free from the thoughts of competition, jealousy, greed, anger and attachment. These are tamasic qualities that hinder our development and affect negatively our mind. Many lead an extremely stressful life due to greed (*lobha*). In the process of gaining more money, power and goods of comfort, they forget to live. They attain everything but peace and happiness. These are the factors that contribute to many ailments. In this process, there is overuse of senses and mind, there is oppression of life with anti-life activities and ultimately the great faculty given to us by nature— the human mind gets affected. With the alternative sattvic way of living, not only can we avoid senility, we can enhance our quality of life and achieve much more.

8

Prevention with Dosha Balance, Food and Home Remedies

Dosha balance

The key feature for the prevention of any ailment lies in our effort to maintain good health in all dimensions. Absence of ailments does not mean good health. A healthy person in the holistic sense is one who is mentally and physically balanced and has a high energy level. For that, one needs to have tremendous sensitivity towards oneself and endeavour to bring the body and mind to balance immediately after a divergence from the state of optimum health. In modern times, human beings lead a 'disconnected' life. When they feel unwell, they do not analyse the causes that may be related to their lifestyle and food habits. They live disassociated from their bodies and do not feel responsible for reverting the state of being unwell to a dynamic state. They depend upon the medical system, which unfortunately provides help only when you have objective symptoms of an ailment proven by numerous tests with highly sophisticated machines. There is no help for the state of being unwell with only subjective symptoms.

According to the age-old wisdom of Ayurveda, the state of being unwell is generally due to the imbalance of the three energies or doshas. This is a state when you do not have objective symptoms of an ailment but if you leave this unattended, it will give rise to an ailment or disorder. Thus, for preventing ailments, an intervention is required immediately to revert to the state of balance. In Ayurvedic terminology, it is the state of prakriti (a natural state of being healthy with the balance of the three energies) and vikriti (state of being unwell due to imbalance). In normal circumstances, the vikriti comes back to prakriti by itself if we live in rhythm with the principles of nature. This phenomenon is easier during youth than childhood and old age and its rapidity also depends upon your fundamental energy level called ojas in Ayurveda. Ojas is the immunity and vitality of the body, which one can increase by taking specific products in the form of nourishment and food supplements. I sum up below some general precautions that you should take for maintaining the body balance and for having more vitality and immunity for avoiding dementia.

+ Eat timely and nourishing meals and do not take anything between two meals. Never over-eat or eat before the previous meal is digested, drink water or some other appetising beverage before meals but not with meals. Each meal should be holistic with vegetables, fruits, grains and spices. The meals should be warm and should contain some fluid items like a soup at least once a day. Nourishing oneself with cold meals should be avoided. Have your dinner at least two hours before going to bed and leave a gap of 10 to 12 hours between dinner and breakfast.

+ To give your system a little rest, observe a semi-fast day once a week. Take light food without salt and without grains. Take fruits, nuts, yoghurt or milk in the morning or for the midday meal and a plate of mixed vegetables and potatoes for dinner. Do not eat onions, garlic, eggs and meat.

92

+ For a regular purification and detoxification of the body, drink every morning about 300 ml of hot water immediately after getting up. Ensure that you pass stools at least once a day or better still twice. Take a mild purgative like senna or sanaye (*Cassia augustifolia*) leaves once a month in a small quantity for purifying your system. Take light food like carrot or pumpkin soups and preparations with semolina after this purification and take warm drinks.

+ Do yoga or other exercise or a walk after drinking hot water in the morning. Yogic exercise comprising of twelve different postures, called *suryapranam* or salutation to the sun is recommended 12 times daily. It takes only about 12 minutes.

+ Keep your body supple with various oils. Creams only protect the skin but oils are absorbed in the body and provide strength to muscles and bones. Once a week a head massage or *champi* is extremely beneficial for calming down brain and nerves.

+ Dosha imbalance can also be in some specific part of the body. For example, if you get moist hands and feet, it is the kapha imbalance; dryness in some specific parts of the body denotes vata imbalance and sweating on a particular part signifies pitta imbalance. In the present context, if you sweat a lot on your forehead and/or also have a burning sensation in hot weather, you need to treat this by anointing, or what is called *lepa* in Ayurveda. Apply sandalwood paste or healing earth on your forehead. Healing earth is a kind of fine clay. One can also use neutral henna (without colour) for this purpose. Make a paste of any of these substances, smear it on your forehead (or any other part of the body where you sweat or get a burning sensation) and keep it there for about 30 minutes or more before washing. Repeat the process several times a day until you are cured.

🔸 It is important to take one of the rasayanas or rejuvenating product to have optimum vitality and energy. Some recipes for that are given on the following pages.

🔸 If you are over-weight, reduce with exercise and special diet* and not by taking industrial diets and staying hungry. That gives rise to an imbalance of doshas and lowers your immunity and vitality (ojas).

🔸 Lastly, make every effort to remain content and happy. Contentment and happiness is a state of mind which does not depend upon wealth and possessions. A rigid attitude makes one unhappy. Learn to seek pleasure in simple things. One way to do this is to dissolve yourself in the beauty of nature. Let the singing of a bird, flowers in the garden, the forest, the beauty of the moon and the radiance of a sunrise or sunset make you happy. Even during difficult times, try to see the positive side and think of what you can learn from facing a particular challenge. Ayurvedic sages said centuries ago that, the causes of most ailments lie in a discontent and frustrated mental state. As has been said earlier, the state of mind has an effect on the dosha balance and dosha imbalance has an effect on the state of mind. Thus, to maintain balance for health and well being, we have to take into consideration both body and mind.

---

* For more details, refer to my book *Losing Weight with Yoga and Ayurveda*. It is available at www.amazon.com.

Food and Home Remedies

The preventive methods with food and home remedies are based upon strengthening nerves and brain with various products. When I first went to Europe several decades ago, the availability of health food products, herbs, spices, etc., was scarce. I recall from my student days in Paris that there were only two very expensive stores with exotic foods. There were very few health food stores with products of special nourishment and they were also quite costly. It is amazing to see now health promoting products from all over the world and a large variety of exotic foods in normal stores that are sold at a very reasonable price. It is unfortunate that, there is a lack of knowledge about the specificity of these products and mostly the right doses are not taken. For example, the precious pumpkin seeds from Austria and Hungary (the black variety without the hard husk) are available for 20 Euro a kilo. Amongst their many properties, the foremost is to strengthen the brain and nerves. The white pumpkin seeds have the same function but the black variety is more intensive. Pumpkin seed oil is also easily available. An overdose of seeds or oil will cause excessive heat in the body and you will get pimples, hair fall and indigestion.

Pumpkin seeds

There is a fine line between food and medicine in Ayurveda. There are many products amongst the daily used herbs and spices, which are also consumed as preventive medicine or remedies. Remedies are in higher and precise dose as compared to the food and are consumed in a prescribed frequency. As prevention, various products are taken either regularly in low dose or seasonally in the form of many recipes. Pumpkin seeds along with the seeds of cantaloupe (honey dew melon), watermelon and cucumber are put together in equal quantity and are popularly known as 'four for brain' in north-west India. They are consumed in winter due to their heat giving (pitta enhancing) and memory promoting qualities and are integrated in various desserts. I give below a simple way to consume the pumpkin seeds, which are easily available in Europe.

Pumpkin seeds

Dose: Maximum daily dose 15-20 gm of seeds or two teaspoons of oil.

You can add pumpkin seeds or oil to the dishes that you prepare or follow the recipes given below.

With Salad and Soup

Pumpkin seeds can be consumed with salad or soup after roasting them a little. Roast them on a hot pan only for a minute. The addition of pumpkin seeds makes the pumpkin soup even more delicious.

I suggest that you use pumpkin seeds regularly in your diet in one form or the other but paying attention to the daily dose.

Alternatively, you can add a teaspoon of pumpkin seed oil to your salad, soup or any other vegetable or meat preparation.

Carrots with pumpkin seeds

You may prepare this simple recipe for breakfast or as a starter for a main meal.

Ingredients for one portion:

Carrots	2-3 or about 300 gm
Olive oil	2 teaspoons

Pumpkin seeds 2 teaspoons (10 gm)

Wash and cut the carrots in thin round pieces. Roast them in olive oil by stirring constantly until they are little soft. Since they are sliced thin, it should take about 10 minutes. Add the pumpkin seeds and roast them with carrots for another two minutes while stirring constantly.

In this dish, you can enjoy the natural taste of both carrots and pumpkin seeds.

Nuts

Nuts are highly important for both nerves and brain. As children, we were given nuts regularly before and during our examinations. Almonds, walnuts, pine nuts, cashew nuts and pistachio nuts are of great importance. Peanuts are in the second category due to the high quantity of oil in them. Nuts are always taken in a limited quantity and on a regular basis because they are hot in their Ayurvedic nature. Taking too much nuts at once can cause imbalance of pitta giving rise to skin eruptions, blisters in mouth, pimples, etc. I have given below a preparation with nuts, honey and some spices that you can take regularly to strengthen your nerves and brain. According to some Ayurvedic texts, it is said that the honey enhances the medicinal value of food products or remedies multiple times when they are left soaked in it for several days. In Ayurvedic terminology, it is called 'ripening' the product in honey. The preparation given below is not only medicinally beneficial, but also delicious.

In modern medical literature in recent years, there is much talk about eating nuts for health. Scientists have announced the results of their studies, but

97

this knowledge is not specific. We are very precise in Ayurveda. You see in the following recipe that the quantity of the nuts is varied. The much talked about walnuts for brain and their anti-oxidant qualities should be consumed in a very moderate quantity. They have an astringent rasa (anti-oxidant) and when too much is taken, cause vata and pitta imbalance and give rise to blisters in the oral cavity.

Nuts with Honey to Strengthen Brain and Nerves

Almonds	200 gm
Cashew nuts	200 gm
Walnuts	100 gm
Pistachio nuts	50 gm
Pine nuts	50 gm
Cloves	10 gm
Cardamom	10 gm
Pepper	10 gm
Fennel	25 gm
Honey	1 Kg

Buy almonds with the skin. Soak in hot water and leave them over night. Next morning, peel off the skin and let them dry. Take the correct weight of other nuts without their shell. Add all five different nuts in a jar of 2 litres. Remove the pods from cardamom and crush all the spices into powder and mix them with the nuts. Add pure liquid honey on all this and stir them all together for about five minutes. Close the lid and let the nuts 'ripen' in the honey for about a week. Stir them from time to time.

Dose: 1 to 2 tablespoons daily. It is best taken on an empty stomach before breakfast. Remember to chew the nuts properly.

Ayurveda talks of many products that improve memory, like brahmi, aindri, jyotishmati, chiranji, lavender, etc. but the purpose of this book is to provide self-help and not professional help. In fact, these products are generally used for healing persons with mental disorders. Since the aim of this book is prevention, I am limiting myself to products that are easily available all over the world and recipes that are simple to follow.

Brain Strengthening and Memory Promoting Rasayana

Fennel	50 gm
Coriander	50 gm
Liquorice	50 gm
Black pepper	25 gm
Long pepper	25 gm
Cardamom	10 gm
Rose petals	25 gm
Lavender	25 gm
Pomegranate peel	25 gm
Cashew nuts	100 gm
Pumpkin seeds	100 gm
Almonds	100 gm
Chiranji	100 gm

Clean and dry all the ingredients and grind them to a fine powder. Mix the powder with honey to make a paste like consistency. For the above quantity, you may need about 1.5 kilo of honey. If it still remains dry, add more honey. Honey is soaked by the herbal powder and that make the preparation hard. Therefore, keep the preparation over-night in the pot and observe before filling it in jars. If needed, add more honey and stir properly.

Dose: Take a teaspoon every day.

Note: If you cannot find Chiranji abroad, just leave it out. Normally the Indian grocery stores abroad have it or they can order it for you.

Strength Promoting Wheat-Milk

I give below a recipe to prepare wheat-milk that enhances immunity and vitality and is especially good for taking out excessive phlegm from the head region. It is prepared by germinating wheat. It is used for treating sinus problems and for that it has to be taken regularly for thirty days. I suggest that you take it for a week every few months for preventing accumulation of mucous in the head region and for promoting strength. It helps prevent cough and cold if taken during the change of seasons.

At the beginning of germination, grains have the best rejuvenating effect on us. According to the Vedic text, all the hidden power in a dried grain comes to being with the help of the five elements that nature is comprised of. From modern biology we also know that enzymes and growth hormones are optimum at this stage. For getting this stage, you have to simply soak the wheat for about 24 hours in water.

Wheat-Milk Drink

Recipe for one person

Step 1: Preparation for wheat milk

Take the best quality organically grown wheat with small grains. This is called *Dinkel* in German and these are the original seeds of wheat. Make sure that the grains are not old and check the date on the packet. If they are old, they will not germinate. Wash and soak them in hot water and make the water level twice the level of the wheat. Cover it with a thin muslin cloth. You will see that the wheat soaks all the water. After few hours, if you see that wheat needs more water and is drying, add more hot water in small quantity to keep it wet. After about 24 hours, crush this wheat in a mixer. You need to add some water in it to grind properly and extract its starchy part. Pass this mixture through a fine big-sized sieve. Move the contents in the sieve with your hand or a spoon to extract all the wheat milk.

Step two: Preparation of the wheat milk drink

Cow milk	100 ml
Ghee	1 teaspoon
Almonds (chopped)	1 tablespoon
Saffron	a pinch
Candy sugar	2 teaspoons or according to taste

Cook the wheat milk obtained from Step 1 along with ghee by constantly stirring for about five minutes. Add the cow's milk gradually and keep stirring. The wheat milk sticks to the bottom of the pan very quickly if you do not stir well and continuously. Cook for about 5 minutes after it comes to the boil. Add the rest of the ingredients and cook for another minute. It becomes like a thick soup and can be taken for breakfast or after a light dinner as dessert.

However, for treating sinusitis, you have to take it before going to bed and keep warm after that. Continue the treatment for 30 days.

A Rasayana to enhance ojas

This is a rasayana you can use every day to enhance your physical and mental capabilities and to increase your ojas (immunity and vitality). A regular intake of rasayana will save you from various minor ailments and will promote strength and vitality. There are many people who suffer from sexual problems due to fatigue, which can be treated by alleviating fatigue with this preparation or any other similar rasayana. Fatigue makes people lazy and sluggish and they limit themselves to minimum work they need to earn their living. That means they leave out sports, yoga, Pranayama, the activities that make the mind relaxed and lead to mental contentment and happiness. All this leads to a passive individual who wants to rest most of the time to get rid of the fatigue. This leads to a frustrated and discontented mental state. These symptoms give rise to all the precursors of dementia, as we have learnt during the course of this book. Therefore, I highly recommend a regular intake of a good rasayana.

Ojas Enhancing Rasayana

Ingredients:

Ajwain	50 gm
Basil (Tulsi leaves)	25 gm
Big cardamom	25 gm
Black pepper	50 gm
Cinnamon	25 gm
Clove	25 gm

Coriander (Dhaniya)	50 gm
Cumin	50 gm
Dill seeds	25 gm
Dried ginger	50 gm
Fennel	50 gm
Fenugreek (Methi)	25 gm
Liquorice (Mullethi)	50 gm
Long pepper	50 gm
Small cardamom	25 gm
Triphala*	100 gm

Clean and dry everything. Take the cardamoms out of their pods. Powder everything with a coffee grinder or a spice grinder. Large substances like liquorice or dried ginger should be made into small pieces with a stone or iron mortar so that they do not break the knife of the grinder. Pass this powder through a fine strainer and crush the rough pieces again. Pass them through the strainer and discard the contents which are still rough. Mix the powder with honey and stir well. Normally, you will need three times more the volume of honey to the volume of powder. The powder soaks the honey and it becomes a thick mixture.

Dose: Depending on your body weight, take from 1 to 1½ teaspoon every day. In case of fatigue, take a teaspoon twice a day.

---

* *Triphala* is a combination of three Himalayan fruits called *amala, harad* and *baheda*. Pulp of the dried fruits without stone is taken in equal quantities and powdered. For more properties of *triphala* and its use in balancing doshas, please refer to my book *Programming your Life with Ayurveda*.

Note: If you cannot get some of the ingredients, you may leave them out. Your rasayana will still be effective.

An Ojas-enhancing spice mixture

Those of you who are familiar with Ayurveda may consult my book on *Ayurvedic Food Culture and Recipes* for numerous spice mixtures for different recipes. But the readers who wish to use this book without getting into the complexities of Ayurvedic cooking may use the following ojas-enhancing spice mixture in various soups and other food preparations. Besides this spice mixture, use also the seasonal herbs available in your own surroundings in soups and salads.

Ojas Enhancing Spice Mixture

Ingredients:

Ajwain or thyme	50 gm
Black pepper	25 gm
Cardamom	25 gm
Cinnamon	25 gm
Clove	25 gm
Cumin	100 gm
Dill seeds	50 gm
Dried ginger	50 gm
Dried mint leaves	50 gm
Fennel	50 gm
Coriander	50 gm
Long pepper	25 gm

Clean and dry these ingredients and take cardamom out from their pods. Grind all the ingredients together and pass them through a sieve to get the fine powder. Grind once again the contents of the sieve to make them into powder. Keep the spice mixture in a glass bottle.

Use one to two teaspoons of this spice daily in your diverse dishes like soups, vegetables or meats. Use the spice mixture while cooking and not afterwards.

Vata balancing and nerves strengthening tea

We have already discussed the importance of balancing vata and how its chronic imbalance leads to diverse ailments including dementia. After a day's work full of rajas (activities) that obviously leads to slight vata imbalance, I suggest to take the following tea that brings balance of vata and strengthen your nerves. That way, you will not accumulate vata imbalance and your nerves will remain strong and stable.

Vata-balancing and Nerve-strengthening tea

Ingredients:

Black pepper	25 gm
Cardamom	25 gm
Coriander	25 gm
Dried Basil leaves	25 gm
Fennel	50 gm
Liquorice	50 gm
Long pepper	25 gm

Clean, dry and grind these ingredients as described above. Keep the powder in a glass bottle. Take half a teaspoon in 250 ml of water and bring it to boil. Let it boil for about two minutes. Filter with a sieve and take it one hour after your dinner or in the afternoon. Take one to two cups daily.

A word about the products

Those of you who are not familiar with Ayurveda need to know the following:

- Do not buy already powdered ingredients. A coffee grinder or a spice grinder should be used to make fresh powders. Powdered ingredients, if kept for a long time lose their nutritional and medicinal properties.

- Make sure that the ingredients are not old. You can find fresh ingredients at the Indian grocery stores abroad. India being such a highly populated country, enterprising Indians live in all parts of the world. Wherever there are Indians, there are Indian grocery shops, as they cannot live without their food and spices. You can locate them in Google or telephone directories.

- In case you still have difficulty, and you find it hard to do the grinding and preparation job yourself, ask your apothecary to order them for you and prepare them. I know that in Germany they do it.

- Keep up your courage and do not give up. The time taken for yourself is time well invested and you will have multiple returns over your lifetime.

Appendix

Ayurvedic preventive medicine needs a lot of personal efforts. As long as we are not sick, the ailment is just a concept and it sounds abstract to most people. I have observed varied reactions in this context. Some people do not feel inspired to do something as they do not want to deal with the 'trouble not yet come'. There are others who have imprudent ideas like they will never fall sick. Contrary to these, there are others who are fearful of all kinds of ailments and live with an anxiety that they will be the first to succumb, when they hear about any widespread ailment or disorder. They take all kinds of exclusive and expensive products when they read or hear about them in the popular media without much scientific and precise information on these products. Ultimately, their obsessive fear of falling ill does them more harm than good.

I suggest taking a middle path. You follow the preventive methods described in this book to improve the quality of your life and to strengthen yourself. Though this book is written for preventing an age-related disorder, you will see the effect of these instructions immediately in terms of improving the quality of life. This is really the essence of preventive medicine in Ayurveda. We should keep our body's defence system so good, our vitality so high and our mind so pure that the enemy of life (sickness, ailments and disorders) is brought to its knees.

In this whole system of prevention, mind is very important. Yoga is very popular in the world but unfortunately, it is reduced mostly to exercises for health. Yoga is actually the science of the senses, mind and soul. I hope this book will inspire you to work more on yourself with various yogic methods and let your inner being blossom.

Let us all join hands together to make the world a disease-free pleasant place to live!

AUM SHANTI

About Dr. Verma

Along with a doctorate degree in reproduction biology in India, Dr. Verma studied Neurobiology in Paris University and obtained a second doctorate. She pursued advanced research at the National Institutes of Health, Bethesda (USA) and the Max-Planck Institute in Freiburg, Germany. At the peak of her career in medical research in a pharmaceutical company in Germany, she realised that the modern approach to health care is basically fragmented and non-holistic. Besides, we are directing all our efforts and resources to cure disease rather than maintaining health. In response, Dr. Verma founded The New Way Health Organisation (NOW) in 1986 to spread the message of holistic living, preventive methods for health care and to promote the use of mild medicine and various self-help therapeutic measures.

Dr. Verma grew up with a strong familial tradition of Ayurveda with a grandmother who had enormous Ayurvedic wisdom and was a gifted healer. She has studied Ayurveda in the traditional Guru-shishya style with Acharya Priya Vrat Sharma of the Benares Hindu University for 23 years.

Dr. Verma is an ardent researcher and is working hard to compile the living tradition of Ayurveda and spread it in the world through her books and other activities. She has published twenty two books on yoga, Ayurveda, Women and Companionship. The books are published in various languages of the world. Besides, she has published numerous scientific articles. Several other books are in preparation. She lectures extensively, teaches in Europe for several months a year, trains students at her two centres in India and gives radio and television programmes. A film on Ayurveda with her was made by German television in 1995 and was shown in 100 countries, in 130 languages. It was the first film on Ayurveda.

Dr. Verma has founded Charaka School of Ayurveda to train interested people with genuine Ayurvedic education so that they can further impart the knowledge of Ayurvedic way of life and save people from becoming a victim of charlatanry in Ayurveda. Dr. Verma is doing several research projects on medicinal plants and their combination in the form of remedies. She is the founder and chairperson of *The Ayurveda Health Organisation*, which is a charitable trust for distributing and promoting Ayurvedic remedies and yoga therapy in rural areas of India. She does regular lectures and workshops for school children in the rural and remote areas of the Himalayas to promote wisdom of traditional science and medicine. Dr. Verma gives seminars, lectures and teaches in the *Charaka School of Ayurveda* with guru-shishya tradition. She is the Academic Director of the *Charaka Ayurveda and Yoga Academy and Cultural Centre (CAYACC)*.

For more information and contacts for Dr. Verma's school and teaching programme see www.ayurvedavv.com and www.ayurveda-books.com

Dr. Vinod Verma's Publications

1. *Patanjali's Yoga Sutra: A Scientific Exposition* (Published in English, Hindi and German).
2. *Ayurveda for Inner Harmony: Nutrition, Sexual Energy and Healing* (Published in English, German, Italian, French, Romanian and Hindi).
3. *Ayurveda a Way of Life* (Published in English, German, Italian, French, Spanish, Czech, Greek, Portuguese, Slovenian and Hindi).
4. *The Kamasutra for Women* (Published in English [America and India], German, French, Dutch, Romanian, Italian, Portuguese, Slovenian Hindi and Malayalam).
5. *Stress-free Work with Yoga and Ayurveda* (Published in German, English [America and India] and Hindi).
6. *Patanjali and Ayurvedic Yoga* (Published in English, German and Hindi).
7. *Programming Your Life with Ayurveda* (Published in German, French, English, Slovenian and Czech).
8. *Ayurvedic Food Culture and Recipes* (Published in English, German, Czech and Hindi).
9. *Yoga: A Natural Way of Being* (Published in English, German, French, Italian and Hindi).
10. *Companionship and Sexuality (Based on Ayurveda and the Hindu tradition)* (Published in English and German).
11. *Natural Glamour: The Ayurveda Beauty Book* (Published in German, Spanish and English)
12. *Losing and Maintaining Weight with Ayurveda and Yoga* (Published in English, Slovenian and German).
13. *The Timeless Wisdom of Ayurveda: A Scientific Exposition* (Published in English and German)
14. *Prakriti and Pulse: The Two Mysteries of Ayurveda* (Published in German)
15. *Good Food for Dogs: Vegetarian nourishment based on Ayurvedic wisdom* (Published in German and English)
16. *Diet for Losing Weight* (published in German and English)
17. *Aum: The Infinite Energy* (Published in German and English)
18. *Pulse Diagnose in Chinese and Ayurvedic Medicine* (co-author for TCM Dr. Florian Ploberger) (published in German)
19. *Shiva's Secrets for Health and Longevity* (published in German and English)
20. *Healing Hands: The Ayurvedic Massage workbook* (in press)
21. *Prevention of Dementia* (published in German and English)
22. *Ayurveda for Dogs* (published in German)

Himalayan Centre

Lectures, Seminars and Training Programmes
To get detailed information on the Charaka School of Ayurveda as well as our other programmes in India and Europe, visit our websites or email us.

The New Way Health Organisation .NOW.
A-130, Sector 26, Noida 201301, U.P., India
Tel. 0091 (0)120 2527820 or (0) 9873704205 or (0)9412224820
Email: ayurvedavv@yahoo.com
Websites: www.ayurvedavv.com www.books.drvinodverma.com

nymphenburger

Dr. Vinod Verma
Demenz-Prävention
aus der Tradition
des Ayurveda

www.ingramcontent.com/pod-product-compliance
Lightning Source LLC
Chambersburg PA
CBHW071058090426
42737CB00013B/2370